AF753823

OECD Business and Finance Outlook 2019

STRENGTHENING TRUST IN BUSINESS

OECD
BETTER POLICIES FOR BETTER LIVES

This work is published under the responsibility of the Secretary-General of the OECD. The opinions expressed and arguments employed herein do not necessarily reflect the official views of OECD member countries.

This document, as well as any data and any map included herein, are without prejudice to the status of or sovereignty over any territory, to the delimitation of international frontiers and boundaries and to the name of any territory, city or area.

Please cite this publication as:
OECD (2019), *OECD Business and Finance Outlook 2019: Strengthening Trust in Business*, OECD Publishing, Paris, *https://doi.org/10.1787/af784794-en*.

ISBN 978-92-64-50714-2 (print)
ISBN 978-92-64-73177-6 (pdf)
ISBN 978-92-64-69525-2 (HTML)
ISBN 978-92-64-98262-8 (epub)

OECD Business and Finance Outlook
ISSN 2617-2569 (print)
ISSN 2617-2577 (online)

The statistical data for Israel are supplied by and under the responsibility of the relevant Israeli authorities. The use of such data by the OECD is without prejudice to the status of the Golan Heights, East Jerusalem and Israeli settlements in the West Bank under the terms of international law.

Photo credits: Cover © Constantine Johnny/Moment via Getty Images.

Corrigenda to OECD publications may be found on line at: *www.oecd.org/about/publishing/corrigenda.htm*.

© OECD 2019

You can copy, download or print OECD content for your own use, and you can include excerpts from OECD publications, databases and multimedia products in your own documents, presentations, blogs, websites and teaching materials, provided that suitable acknowledgement of OECD as source and copyright owner is given. All requests for public or commercial use and translation rights should be submitted to *rights@oecd.org*. Requests for permission to photocopy portions of this material for public or commercial use shall be addressed directly to the Copyright Clearance Center (CCC) at *info@copyright.com* or the Centre français d'exploitation du droit de copie (CFC) at *contact@cfcopies.com*.

Foreword

This is the fifth edition of the OECD Business and Finance Outlook, an annual publication that presents unique data and analysis on the trends, both positive and negative, that are shaping tomorrow's world of business, finance and investment. Using analysis from a wide range of perspectives, this year's edition considers the importance of public trust in business and finance, offering a conceptual approach to understanding facets of trust in finance, investment and business with respect to economic value, fairness and integrity of conduct, as well as alignment with societal values. The *Outlook* provides an assessment of factors that contributed to a deterioration of trust during the global financial crisis; reviews recent developments that could contribute to a renewed erosion of trust; and, offers policy considerations to help strengthen public trust in business and finance. These findings will contribute to the work of the newly-created OECD Trust in Business Initiative (www.oecd.org/corporate/trust-business.htm).

The *OECD Business and Finance Outlook 2019* is the joint work of staff of the OECD Directorate for Financial and Enterprise Affairs. It has benefited from comments by delegates of relevant committees and other parts of the OECD Secretariat.

The publication was prepared under the supervision of Flore-Anne Messy, based on contributions from Robert Patalano and Caroline Roulet (Chapter 1), Barbara Bijelic, Pablo Antolin, Adele Atkinson and Miles Larbey (Chapter 2), Kathryn Gordon (Chapter 3), Hans Christiansen (Chapter 4), James Mancini, Cristina Volpin and Miles Larbey (Chapter 5).

Table of Contents

Tables

Figures

Boxes

Follow OECD Publications on:

http://twitter.com/OECD_Pubs
http://www.facebook.com/OECDPublications
http://www.linkedin.com/groups/OECD-Publications-4645871
http://www.youtube.com/oecdilibrary
OECD Alerts http://www.oecd.org/oecddirect/

Editorial

Trust underwrites every one of our economic relationships. From everyday commerce to the provision of credit, from long-term investment in infrastructure to the sustainable management of pensions, it is the invisible foundation of a fair and open market.

The 2008 global financial crisis marked a turning point in the way governments considered the role and importance of trust in policymaking. The policy responses to the crisis – unprecedented in their scope and cost – had one underlying goal: to restore trust in the financial sector and the wider business community.

Governments were largely successful in fending off a full-scale global depression, but more than a decade on business has still not fully recovered the trust lost in the crisis. Today, a series of important social, financial and economic trends have placed trust in business and finance once again at the front of mind for political and business leaders alike.

For businesses, trust is imperative to achieving long-term value and profitability. Customers, employees and investors increasingly expect high standards of conduct that go well beyond the letter of the law, and are empowered by information technologies to mobilise when a company's conduct falls short. At the same time, business operations are more global than ever, spanning a patchwork of legal and cultural environments which increase the risk of wrongdoing before the law or public opinion. Fully incorporating the concepts of trust into corporate governance is the only way to truly manage such complex and evolving risks.

In the wider business context, the longer-term impact of many post-crisis reforms remain to be seen, while financial stability and conduct are ongoing concerns. State-owned enterprises have risen in international importance, amplifying the long-standing challenge of balancing public and private-sector concerns. Digital markets have enabled new data-driven business models, where the role of trust is especially important, but may not yet be fully understood or appreciated.

The experience of the crisis still weighs on public sentiment, and these recent developments come at a time when the pillars of prosperity – such as the importance of efficient capital markets, the value of global trade, or the role of corporations – seem uncertain in the eyes of many. Strengthening trust in business is now an urgent challenge, and the OECD is responding with its newly launched *Trust in Business Initiative*.

This latest edition of our annual OECD Business and Financial Outlook, with its focus on strengthening trust in business, is the first outcome of this initiative. It puts forward the empirical rationale for incorporating trust into market governance and business policy settings, and provides a framework for policy makers to do so in reference to global standards and international best practice.

Moving forward, the initiative will further develop the link between trust and business performance; provide a platform for cooperation between governments, business and civil society; build capacity in governments and SOEs; and forge the kind of partnerships between the public and private sectors needed to move the dial.

The *Trust in Business Initiative* represents a new phase in the OECD's long-standing focus on restoring trust, and underscores the Organisation's commitment to fostering businesses practices and markets that are worthy of the public's confidence, and properly reflect the ever-changing expectations and demands of the 21st century.

Greg Medcraft

Director, OECD Directorate for Financial and Enterprise Affairs

Why trust is important in business and finance

Following the global financial crisis, public trust in governments, corporates, financial markets and financial institutions declined as societies in many part of the world experienced an erosion of economic well-being. As governments used unprecedented policy tools – including monetary, fiscal, regulatory, structural measures– to restore stability and growth, surveys have shown evidence of a gradual improvement in public trust.

However, more than a decade after the crisis, major economies are at a crossroads. Despite moderate growth across OECD countries, business and investment activities have been anaemic, and markets are increasingly vulnerable to downside risks. While progress has been made on financial reforms, implementation has been uneven. New concerns have arisen regarding competition, consumer protection, and privacy in digital markets. Many are questioning the extent to which post-crisis growth has been sustainable, fair, and inclusive, and whether investment and business practices are aligned with societal values, such as social and environmental issues. Strengthened public trust in business and finance will be important to encouraging the productive investment and commerce that contribute to inclusive and sustainable economic growth.

This introduction offers a perspective on public trust as it relates to business and finance. The first part briefly looks at the academic literature on public trust; the second part reflects on OECD work on trust in institutions and in business; and the third part offers a framework for considering trust in business and finance.

Perspectives on public trust in business and finance

Trust is a basic element for the well-functioning of institutions, including governments, markets, businesses, and for society more broadly. The concepts of public trust have been considered by a range of authors, including by Kenneth Arrow, Douglass North, Francis Fukuyama, and Robert Putnam, among others, who explore the importance of public trust for the functioning of institutions, markets, and commerce (see Arrow, 1999; Fukuyama, 1995; Putnam, 2000). Arrow suggests that virtually every commercial transaction has within itself an element of trust, as transactions conducted over a period of time have an element of uncertainty. He argues that much of the economic backwardness in the world can be explained by the lack of mutual confidence (Arrow, 1972). Fukuyama illustrates how societies with high social capital from public trust are more able to efficiently pool resources – labour, capital, ideas and innovations – to generate economic growth and progress, have low levels of corruption, and maintain level playing fields.

By contrast, low social capital societies tend to have lower non-government capital formation, less efficient markets and financial services, more corruption, and more costs associated with these inefficiencies that dampen the entrepreneurial forces for economic gains. Reflections on trust and society suggest that where social and legal mechanisms for the efficient resolution of principal-agent conflicts are weak– i.e. where most potential pairs of economic transactors cannot trust each other– the private returns to production fall (Knack, 2015). In this regard, North argued that the inability of societies to develop effective, low-cost enforcement of contracts is the most important source of both historical stagnation and contemporary underdevelopment in some parts of the world (North, 1990).

According to Hawley and Kirby, trust in institutions (including corporations) derives from the capacity of these institutions to fulfil a commitment (Hawley, 2014), pp.1-20; Kirby et al., 2018), pp.75-129). Three observations are relevant to qualify trust in the financial system and commerce. First, some commitments are explicit while others are implicit, and eliciting implicit commitments is required to build trust. Second, some commitments are legally enforceable, while others are not. It follows that, while compliance matters, restoring or enhancing trust requires moving beyond compliance. Third, trust combines different levels of aggregation, from the trustworthy corporation to trust in a particular industry (e.g. the financial system) and trust in a set of social institutions (including government). From these conceptual studies, one can infer that the sharp deterioration of public trust in governments and private-sector institutions that engage in capital formation and commerce calls for the careful consideration of possible policy responses and actions.

The OECD's perspective

The OECD has engaged in measurements of public trust in government, public policy and more recently in business and digitalisation. The work on measuring public trust highlights that only a society where people cooperate with one another, and where public institutions act competently and are widely accessible to citizens, enables a higher quality of life for all. Trust in other people and trust in institutions are essential ingredients for social and economic progress, while a prospering society, in turn, is one in which trust can flourish (OECD, 2017a).

OECD (2017a) defines trust as a person's belief that another person or institution will act consistently with their expectations of positive behaviour. The same publication highlights that trust in institutions requires that they are "competent and effective in delivering on their goals, that they operate consistently with a set of values that reflect citizens' expectations of integrity and fairness", and is also dependent on the extent to which they align with business ethics and broader societal expectations. Underpinning these expectations is the distinction between rational trust, such as in strategic outcomes related to anticipated economic benefits, and moralistic trust, based on shared beliefs and norms of the individuals and societies doing the trusting (see Uslander, 2008 and Fukuyama, 1995). In particular, trust is critically important because it is: necessary to increase the confidence of investors and consumers; essential for key economic activities; and, is important for the success of many government policies, programmes and regulations that depend on cooperation and compliance of citizens. Appropriate government policies, including monetary, fiscal and structural policies, regulations, law, and enforcement are vital to establish formal behaviours that promote and reinforce trust.[1]

A trust framework for business and finance

In light of differing perspectives on public trust in various facets of societal engagement, a simple framework for structuring the elements of public trust related to business and finance is needed to better explore the relevance of trust in markets and business, where they may be fragile, and what can be done to strengthen them. The OECD descriptions of trust can be applied to stakeholders that are narrowly defined as participants in the financial and commercial transactions, including those that supply, demand, and intermediate capital or commercial exchanges, or defined broadly with respect to societal expectations of behaviours and outcomes. Expectations of well-functioning arenas of business and finance would include: (i) effectiveness in ensuring predictability in engagement that yields economic benefit; (ii) that the exchange of those benefits is fair, and conducted with integrity; and, (iii) that behaviours pursued by participants in business and finance are aligned with ethical standards and societal values. They would include a disposition to fulfil a broader set of commitments, explicit (such as the ones above) or implicit, be they legally enforceable or not.[2]

The predictability of economic and normative behaviours are equally relevant for individual participants and the public at large. Individual participants in markets and business generally expect economic returns within a range established by historical precedence, and they might seek to achieve such benefits through trust in established norms of behaviours set by laws, regulatory guidance, or industry standards. Furthermore, given ample room for judgement within these explicit perimeters of engagement, participants would expect others to act with high ethical standards and in a manner that strengthens trust in this engagement.

Societal trust in finance and business rests upon expectations that these activities will contribute to sustainable and inclusive economic growth; will not lead to imposition of losses on society through excessive risk taking; and will be aligned with broader societal values related to environmental, social, and labour, among other issues.[3] To this end, one may argue that public trust in business considers the degree to which the public believes that business will act in a particular manner by which the business has included the public's interest into its own.[4] In this respect, evidence suggests that sustainable economic growth from well-functioning markets and business most often fosters greater opportunity, tolerance and diversity, social mobility, commitment to fairness, and dedication to democracy (Friedman, 2005). Mutually reinforcing behaviours have the potential to contribute to a virtuous cycle between sustainable and inclusive economic growth and trust. By contrast, the global financial crisis illustrated that when excessive risk-taking and skewed rewards contributed to unsustainable and exclusionary growth, public trust was impaired.

The following trust matrix illustrates core elements of trust between individual participants in business and finance, and the general public, using the core elements with respect to economic value, fairness and conduct, and integrity of behaviours that align with societal benefits. Of course, the relative strength of these expectations would depend on type of business and finance cultures in each jurisdiction, the level of formal state involvement in the economy, and societal values, among other factors. The tolerance for loss within the financial sector, to individuals and society, would depend in part on the formal state intervention in the economic regime, and circumstances. Also, the fairness and conduct would depend on society's acceptance of formal rules of engagement, such as to protect investors and consumers, or to ensure level playing field, which may set perimeters for economic gain and risks. Lastly, values alignment, which reflects behaviours aligned with moral and ethical principles distinct from formal laws and regulations, is associated with positive or negative impact of spillovers related to, for example, business culture, or considerations related to environmental or social impact.

Portions of the matrix are reflected in each chapter of the 2019 OECD Business and Finance Outlook and collectively the chapters cover all elements of the matrix. This gives a full picture of the ways in which behaviours in business and finance could undermine trust, and how to address them.

Table 1. Trust matrix

	Economic Value	Fairness, Conduct, and Integrity	Values Alignment
Participants (narrow)[1]	Predictability of general market and asset class performance and liquidity, such that participants can expect to receive investment outcomes relative to risks in a range of historical outcomes. Predictability of commercial behaviours through traditional and digital markets. Expectations of macroeconomic and macrofinancial policies conducive to stable growth that promotes investment and commercial benefits.	Expectation that behaviours align with established and explicit rules of acceptable conduct, which promote fair treatment, transparency, adherence to laws.	Behaviours that strive to achieve best practices beyond adherence and compliance, and which contribute to the reputation of the industry. Business cultures that promote behaviours and outcomes that align with societal values.
Society (broad)[2]	Expectation that the aggregation of market and commercial behaviours results in economic benefits to society, through sustainable and inclusive growth, without the socialisation of losses to society.	Expectation that policies and oversight of rules of conduct ensure sufficient fairness, a level playing field, and tolerated conduct to ensure integrity of markets and commerce. Expectation that there is a competent enforcement mechanism in place to minimise egregious breaches.	Behaviours that are widely considered to be positive for societal well-being beyond the economic sphere. Alignment of business and finance sector behaviours with environmental, social, and governance factors, among others.

Notes:

This guiding framework reflects elements of OECD work on trust, directly or indirectly, in its various divisions. The purpose of the framework is to provide a unifying conceptual approach that incorporates key elements of trust in finance and business, and to help readers understand how the chapters in this publication are interrelated.

1. Participants include:"
   - both those involved in the financial and commercial transactions and institutions that oversee the fairness, conduct and integrity of activities.
   - retail and institutional investors who provide capital, issuers that demand capital, and enablers such as market intermediaries (traders, funds, vehicles, and exchanges).
   - consumers and providers of goods and services that engage through traditional and digital exchanges.

2. Societal trust may differ from participants' trust because societies may judge not just the behaviours but also the aggregate outcomes and their impact on society, such as with respect to social and environmental issues. When desired outcomes are not sufficiently achieved, citizens may call upon public policy to change the rules related to economic value, fairness and integrity. For example, current societal frustration with the effects of globalisation with respect to the distribution of economic gains is influencing populist movements that are challenging the current institutions and rules related to multilateralism.

Notes

[1] OECD trends and surveys point to six areas where trust in institutions can be improved: reliability, responsiveness, openness, integrity and fairness, better regulation and inclusive policymaking. See OECD (2017b).

[2] According to Kirby et al. (2018), such a disposition particularly matters under specific circumstances, in particular when there is a need to preserve systemic trust and where corporate political power can undermine a state's legitimacy.

[3] The key distinction between the market participant and society, which includes market participants, is that the trust of society is not necessarily predicated upon direct engagement in markets and commerce; societal expectations exist distinct from direct engagement and benefit with commercial and financial transaction.

[4] Adapted from Financial Times Lexicon, see FT website.

References

Arrow, K.J. (1999), "Observations on Social Capital. In Dasgupta", P., Serageldin, I. (Eds), Social Capital. A Multifaceted Perspective. Washington: The World Bank, http://documents.worldbank.org/curated/en/663341468174869302/Social-capital-a-multifaceted-perspective.

Arrow, K.J. (1972), "Gifts and exchanges", Philosophy and Public Affairs, Vol. 1/4, https://www.jstor.org/stable/pdf/2265097.pdf.

Friedman, B. (2005), *The Moral Consequences of Economic Growth,* Alfred A. Knopf New York, isbn=0679448918.

Fukuyama, F. (1995), "Trust: Social Virtues and the Creation of Prosperity", *International Journal on World Peace*, https://www.jstor.org/stable/20752121.

Hawley K. (2014), Trust, distrust and commitments, *Noûs*, 48(1), pp.1-20, https://doi.org/10.1111/nous.12000.

Kirby N., A. Kirton and A. Crean (2018), "Do corporations have a duty to be trustworthy?", *Journal of the British Academy*, 6(s1), pp.75-129.

Knack, S. (2015), "Trust, Associational Life and Economic Performance," prepared for the HRDC-OECD International Symposium on The Contribution of Investment in Human and Social Capital to Sustained Economic Growth and Well-Being.

OECD (2017a), *OECD Guidelines on Measuring Trust*, OECD Publishing, Paris, https://doi.org/10.1787/9789264278219-en.

OECD (2017b), "Trust and Public Policy: How Better Governance Can Help Rebuild Public Trust", in *OECD Public Governance Reviews*, OECD Publishing, Paris, https://doi.org/10.1787/9789264268920-en.

Putnam, R, (2000), *Bowling Alone: The Collapse and Revival of American Community*, Simon & Schuster, New York, ISBN: 978-0684832838.

Uslander (2010), "Trust and the Economic Crisis of 2008", *Corporate Reputation Review*, https://doi.org/10.1057/crr.2010.8.

Abbreviations and acronyms

ABCP	asset backed commercial paper
ACSI	Australian Council of Superannuation Investors
AI	authorised institution
AIMA	Alternative Investment Management Association
APIs	application program interfaces
APs	authorised participants
ASIC	Australian Securities and Investments Commission
BIAC	Business and Industry Advisory Committee to the OECD
BRRD	Bank Recovery and Resolution Directive
CDO	collateralised debt obligation
CLO	collateralised loan obligation
CoCo	contingent convertible
DB	defined benefit (a pension arrangement where benefits are linked through a formula to the members' wages or salaries, length of employment, or other factors.)
DC	defined contribution (pension plans to which fixed contributions are paid and there are no legal or constructive obligations for the sponsor to pay further contributions in the event of unfavourable plan experience.)
DEA	direct electronic access
EBITDA	earnings before interest, taxes, depreciation, and amortization
ECB	European Central Bank
EM	Emerging market
EME	Emerging market economy
ESG	environmental, social and governance
ETF	exchange traded fund
EU	European Union

FCA	Financial Conduct Authority
FCPA	Foreign Corrupt Practices Act
FDI	foreign direct investment
FinCoNet	International Network on Financial Consumer Protection
FSB	Financial Stability Board
FX	Forex
G20	Group of 20 (Argentina, Australia, Brazil, Canada, China, France, Germany, India, Indonesia, Italy, Japan, Mexico, Russia, Saudi Arabia, South Africa, Korea, Turkey, the United Kingdom, United States and the European Union)
GDP	gross domestic product
GDPR	General Data Protection Regulation
GT	gross tonnage
HFT	high-frequency trading
IAASB	International Auditing and Assurance Standards Board
ICT	information and communication technology
IESBA	International Ethics Standards Board for Accountants
IFAC	International Federation of Accountants
IFSWF	International Forum of Sovereign Wealth Funds
IMF	International Monetary Fund
IOSCO	International Organization of Securities Commissions
MAS	Monetary Authority of Singapore
MiFID	Markets in Financial Instruments Directive
OECD	Organisation for Economic Co-operation and Development
PAYG	pay-as-you-go (Unfunded pension plans that are financed directly from contributions from the plan sponsor or provider and/or the plan participant.)
PPP	public-private partnership
PRI	Principles for Responsible Investment
PTF	principal trading firms
RBC	Responsible Business Conduct

S&P 500	Standard & Poor's 500-stock index
SDGs	sustainable development goals
SEC	Securities and Exchange Commission
SIV	structured investment funds
SME	small and medium-sized enterprise
SOE	state-owned enterprise
STOXX 600	The STOXX Europe 600 Index is derived from the STOXX Europe Total Market Index (TMI).
TUAC	Trade Union Advisory Committee to the OECD
WTO	World Trade Organization

Executive summary

Trust is a basic element for the well-functioning of institutions, including governments, markets and businesses, and for society more broadly. In the decade since the global financial crisis, many policies and initiatives have been designed to help restore trust at national and global levels. However, the backlashes against globalisation and mounting protectionism trends mean that questions remain about whether enough has been done by public and private stakeholders to support healthy trust in the financial and business landscape. And, if not, what can be done to address remaining concerns?

Against this backdrop, the 2019 OECD Business and Finance Outlook explores how to strengthen public trust in business and finance, to support economic and societal well-being. The *Outlook* looks at five perspectives that, while non-exhaustive, provide policy makers with concrete considerations for action. These perspectives include a focus on trust and: financial markets (Chapter 1); financial institutions—such as banks and pension funds (Chapter 2); company liability—that is, trust in companies to obey the law (Chapter 3); the level playing field, focusing on the rising importance of state-owned enterprises (SOEs) and their associated conduct risks (Chapter 4); and online markets (Chapter 5).

Trust in financial markets

The *Outlook* considers potential risks that could erode trust in the financial sector in the future. These risks include, for example, the abundant issuance of sovereign, corporate and bank debt, which has supported post-crisis growth but has raised concern over potential risks of excessive debt as the credit cycle matures. The *Outlook* also considers financial market developments and innovations—including high-frequency trading and crypto-assets—that can make financial markets both more efficient and inclusive, but also exposes them to volatility and loss.

To strengthen trust in financial markets, policy makers should target financial authorities' ability to identify and mitigate risk in their management of public debt and in ensuring the liquidity of the financial system, for example through the greater use of tail-risk stress scenarios. Market-based finance could also benefit from more consistent implementation of FSB/IOSCO recommendations, in order to improve liquidity risk management in investment funds. Greater assessment of the impact and risks of algorithmic and high-frequency trading strategies during periods of market stress should also be undertaken, in order to reduce the likelihood that flash crashes occur and result in market contagion.

Trust in financial institutions

Population ageing, low returns on retirement savings, low growth, less stable employment careers, and insufficient pension coverage among some groups of workers: These trends have eroded the belief that pension systems are managed with workers' best interests in mind and that they will deliver on their promises, once workers reach retirement age.

The *Outlook* considers three policy objectives to win back trust in financial institutions: promoting prudent pension management and supporting pension funds' fiduciary duties; enhancing financial consumer protection; and addressing environmental and social risks.

A starting point in this regard is strengthened implementation and enforcement of existing OECD policy instruments, such as the OECD Core Principles of Private Pension Regulation, the G20 High Level Principles on Financial Consumer Protection, and the OECD Guidelines for Multinational Enterprises. Policy responses in this respect must also adequately address the challenges of increasing digitalisation, as well as the need to align financial institutions with societal duties, such as the integration of ESG factors in investment strategies.

Trust and corporate liability

A key pillar of trust in business is the belief that companies conduct their operations —at a minimum—in compliance with the law. This trust is built in two ways: First, companies need to take steps to prevent unlawful activity from occurring. Second, if there are suspicions of unlawful conduct, companies should take steps to report these suspicions to law enforcement authorities and to cooperate in the resolution of the matter.

Governments have a key role to play in establishing the framework conditions for these actions. This includes establishing and effectively implementing a robust corporate liability framework, with effective incentives for cooperation. Progress has been made: Over the 20 years since the Anti-Bribery Convention entered into force, Parties to the Convention have introduced corporate liability for foreign bribery and, more recently, compliance incentives. At the global level, further efforts should be made to collaborate on and harmonise country-by-country corporate liability systems, given the increasing number and complexity of multijurisdictional corporate crime cases.

Trust and the level playing field

The importance of SOEs in domestic and global markets is on the rise. An effective policy response to SOEs' heightened exposure to corruption risk is necessary to build trust and ensure a level playing field for business. OECD data indicates that SOEs are uniquely exposed to corruption risk: SOEs active in certain sectors – notably steel production – tend to be less profitable than private peers, yet less likely to go out of business. Similarly, SOEs have a higher risk of engaging in certain forms of corruption. They are also less likely than private companies to divest from certain projects or disengage from business partners, due to integrity concerns.

To address the potential SOE 'trust deficit', governments must hold SOEs equally liable—both at home and abroad—to anti-corruption and integrity legal, regulatory, and policy frameworks. In so doing, policy makers should focus on raising transparency, improving investment regulation related to state ownership, and fighting corruption in SOEs. These directions reflect the policy advice in the recently adopted and G20-endorsed OECD Guidelines on Anti-Corruption and Transparency in SOEs.

Public trust in online markets

Online markets offer a host of benefits for consumers through new and cheaper products. However, online markets can only fulfil their potential if they benefit from consumer trust. Where product information is hard to obtain and assess, markets may not respond to consumers' needs. Consumers may be forced to rely on imprecise indicators of quality—such as brand names—to establish trust. This, in turn, limits firms' incentives to improve their offering and deters new entrants. In other cases, consumers may be deterred from using online markets altogether.

Establishing an environment of trust in online markets requires multidisciplinary (and likely cross-border) approaches from authorities charged with ensuring fair competition, consumer protection, and data protection, as well as other regulators. Both enforcement and advocacy efforts are necessary to ensure that consumers are given meaningful opportunities to make choices in online markets, and in so doing stimulate competition in order to get the best deal possible.

Chapter 1. Trust and financial markets

This chapter considers trust in financial markets by exploring factors that contribute to public trust in markets, post-crisis developments that have contributed to help ameliorate the loss in public trust provoked by the financial crisis, and potential risks to the financial sector that could erode trust in the future. The chapter considers developments in sovereign, corporate and bank debt markets, and the potential for unexpected losses from high leverage in less benign macro and market conditions. It also explores the growth and benefits of market-based finance, and considers whether structural features of certain products could contribute to market risks and amplification of stress in less liquid fixed-income markets.

1.1. Framing the importance of trust in financial markets

1.1.1. Public trust in markets

The introduction to the Business and Finance Outlook has highlighted the importance of public trust in institutions and participants in market economies to support sustainable and inclusive growth. Financial markets across OECD countries and many other jurisdictions are essential to facilitate efficient allocation of capital to the real economy, either directly or through intermediaries. For savers, financial markets provide higher long-term risk-adjusted returns than bank deposits, allowing for the accumulation of wealth. For governments, companies, and households, issuance of capital provides an efficient alternative to bank borrowing that underpins short-term working capital needs and long-term fixed investment in infrastructure and business expansion. **As financial markets are the primary mechanism to intermediate between investors and economic actors, public trust in markets is vital to its role to effectively and efficiently convert savings into productive economic growth, and in turn to reward capital providers with long-term returns commensurate with risks.**

As well, the behaviour of institutions and participants in markets is critically important to maintaining society's trust in markets, and forms a distinct component of investor confidence.[1] In this regard, public trust in markets is broader than investor optimism in the delivery of adequate risk-adjusted returns, as it extends to the public's expectation that markets will serve sustainable economic growth and contribute to the well-being of society (economic, ethical and otherwise) in various forms.

Thus, sound oversight and regulation of markets and market participants, and of the stability of the financial system, are key factors in maintaining trust in markets, because they help ensure an appropriate balance of risk and returns for efficient functioning and sustainable flows between investors and consumers of capital. In addition, the transparency and integrity of markets is important to ensure fairness across myriad participants. As such, shocks that expose macrofinancial imbalances, excesses in risk taking, malfunctioning of financial innovations, and ineffective oversight often contribute to a sharp deterioration of trust in the financial system. Moreover, shocks in markets that erode the sustainability and inclusiveness of economic growth, can compound distrust in the financial system.

For these reasons, **the Global Financial Crisis caused public trust in financial markets to decline sharply amid the heavy market losses on both traditional and complex financial products.** In response, from policy makers engaged in efforts to craft a coordinated global policy response across affected countries by providing a liquidity backstop for the financial system, highly accommodative monetary policies across OECD countries, recapitalisation of core banks and other large financial institutions, and targeted central bank programmes to restore intermediation through markets. Over the post-crisis period, improving market conditions and the continuation of efforts to address the faultiness of the crisis through regulatory reforms have gradually improved public trust. Nevertheless, by some measures it remains fairly low, which calls for policy makers' attention.

To the extent that surveys showing rising trust from low levels is indicative of public sentiment, trust in financial services has increased in most of the surveyed countries over the past several years (Figure 1.1; Edelman, 2018). This raises a question as to the extent trust is merely rising on market buoyancy and liquidity resulting from highly accommodative monetary policy, and the extent to which public trust could withstand the materialisation of major risks, particularly in areas that were meant to have been addressed by the post-crisis regulatory reforms.

Figure 1.1. Public trust in financial services, 2012-2018

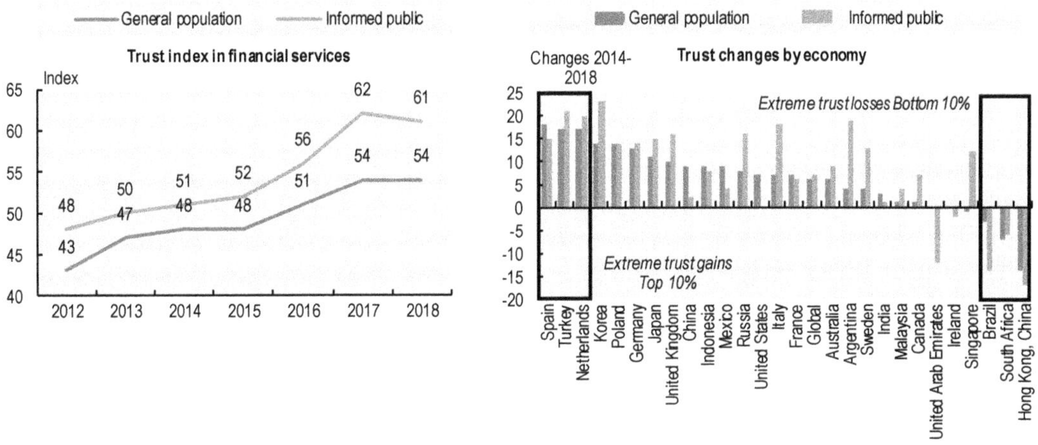

Source: 2018 Edelman Trust Barometer, OECD calculations.

1.1.2. Conceptual framework for assessing how trust could impact markets and economic growth

In order to better assess trust and markets, a working definition has been developed to evaluate the elements of trust related to investors, market intermediaries, and the public.

Framework. A conceptual framework for assessing how trust could impact markets must balance the perspectives of the individual investor and the public at large. In this regard the concept of trust in the markets differs from aspects of investor confidence related to conditions that maximise short-term returns based on assessment of economic and business fundamentals.

For the individual investor, trust may take several forms, including:

- predictability of behaviours (based on historical experience) from markets that are efficient, open, stable and sound, and result in returns commensurate with risks;
- confidence that the rules and oversight of market interactions support the soundness, fairness and integrity of markets;[2] and,
- that, both within and beyond the established rules, market participants' behaviours will be ethical in serving the interests of customers.

The public at large also has a fundamental trust relationship with the markets that is distinct from market participants.[3] Public trust is built on the premise that markets serve a purpose that is beneficial to societies, directly in terms of supporting sustainable economic growth, and also indirectly through positive spillovers to other stakeholders. In addition, trust can be further strengthened when behaviours of markets are aligned with broader societal values, such as those related to environmental, social and governance objectives (see Chapter 2). In this respect, trust is built on mutually reinforcing behaviours that markets contribute to sustainable economic growth in its broadest sense to support societal wellbeing. When this relationship breaks down, such as when market crises impose losses that are borne by taxpayers, or when deflating asset bubbles contribute to widespread losses, public trust can be eroded by market failures. To varying degrees, there are societal expectations that market participants should behave in a manner that does not compromise broader societal values.

Furthermore, the integrity of markets, through governance and conduct, help keep them sound and fair in the eyes of market participants. For this reason, the public expects that egregious losses would not be imposed on portions of society due to malfunctioning markets, such as through types of investment products. As well, market participants expect that market innovations through products, services, and technologies – once their adoption reaches a material level – are properly regulated in a manner proportional to potential risks, and with adequate protections and financial education for financial consumers.

Scope of assessment. With these elements of trust in mind, the next sections of the chapter consider developments in the post crisis era relative to three areas of the markets that have experienced substantial developments. They include:

- **Global markets' intermediation of sovereign and corporate debt (section 2),** which has contributed to the growth of sovereign and corporate debt to unprecedented levels through the fixed-income markets.
- **Growth of market-based finance (section 3),** resulting from very strong growth in investment funds and some forms of securitisation.
- **Innovations in financial technologies (section 4)** has great promise to increase the availability of products, improve cost efficiencies, and transaction speed, and enhance transparency and security through blockchain.[4]

These three developments have occurred in both advanced and emerging markets across the world, although the extent varies across countries. When normalisation of monetary policies occur in OECD economies, it will contribute to a repricing of traded debt across global markets. Debt held in market-based vehicles, from funds to securitisations, have yet to be tested by a sharp change in market pricing and shifting investor demands, which could uncover structural fragilities. As well, while innovative financial technologies continue to bring benefits to financial consumers through cost and operational efficiencies, in some ways they could contribute to disruptive changes or amplify risks during periods of market stress. These sections explore how risks, if not addressed, could cause market disruptions and unpredictable distributions of loss that could erode public trust in markets. The final section offers policy considerations to address aspects of the markets where potential risks could undermine trust.

1.2. Rising debt in fixed-income markets

This section considers the rise of sovereign, corporate and contingent convertible bank debt through fixed-income markets across advanced and emerging market economies in the post-crisis era. It assesses factors that contributed to the rise of debt, benefits of market access at low financing costs, and potential risks that could undermine public trust in financial markets and related policies.

1.2.1. Sovereign debt markets

In the decade following the crisis, outstanding debt in sovereign debt markets has grown considerably, and now stands at historically high levels in many advanced and emerging market economies. The post-crisis strategy pursued by many governments to increase fiscal deficits to boost stimulus contributed to a rise of global sovereign debt from 62% of GDP in 2008 to a peak of 83% in 2017 (Figure 1.2).

The rise in sovereign debt in many countries marked a coordinated global response to the global financial crisis and, subsequently, the European crisis. Fiscal stimulus in nearly all OECD countries was pursued through discretionary measures in response to the crisis, to prevent the downturn from gathering momentum and to support a sustainable economic recovery (OECD, 2009).

There is ample evidence of the positive effects of such stimulus, in concert with monetary policy accommodation, to stabilise economic and financial market conditions, and even to support improved corporate profitability.[5]

At the same time, possible longer-term concerns were raised over the negative consequences of high debt through sovereign debt markets (Freedman et al., 2010); Auerbach et al., (2017). Evidence at the time showed that adverse reactions in financial markets are likely in response to higher government debt and that such reactions may depend on the initial budget situation OECD, 2009).

While debt-to-GDP has recently stabilised in at least some OECD countries due to moderate economic growth, the nominal debt level remains at an all-time peak of USD 64 trillion. The key risk of very high sovereign debt is that repayments could become unsustainable, either due to resource or political constraints. However, even where debt is high but sustainable from the issuer's perspective, investor perceptions of risk could drive market costs much higher in the case that large amounts of maturating debt needs to be refinanced.[6] In turn, this could raise the price of debt across all domestic issuers, including local governments, corporates, and households.

Figure 1.2. Sovereign outstanding debt for selected economies, 2000-2018

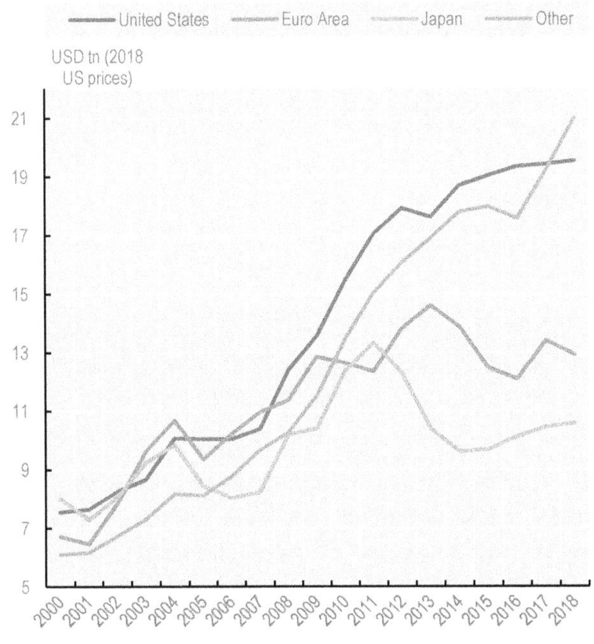

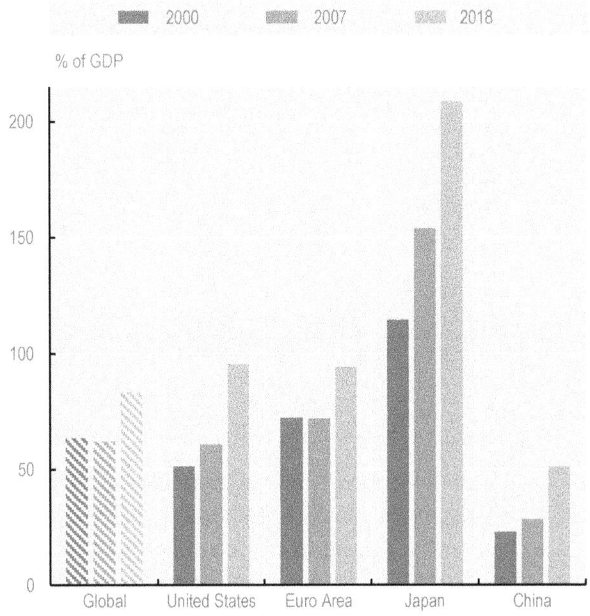

Note: The financial instruments covered comprise currency and deposits (which are mostly zero in the case of credit to the private non-financial sector), loans and debt securities. The sum of these three instruments is defined here as "core debt". For the government sector, core debt generally represents the bulk of total debt. Debt data for 63 countries are used in this chart. Outstanding amounts are presented in 2018 USD adjusted by US Consumer Price Index.

Source: Bank of International Settlements, Credit to the non-financial sector database, OECD calculations.

Prior periods of rising sovereign debt and deficit spending have increased the market cost of credit to compensate for additional risks and, at very high levels of debt and deficits, can lead to a loss of investor confidence and very high risk premia across fixed income markets. These phenomena can be seen clearly in the Latin American debt crisis, European peripheral sovereign-banking crisis earlier this decade, and several Asian countries during the Asian financial crisis (Reinhart and Rogoff, 2008), when these developments have morphed into more widespread market concerns.

The growth of sovereign debt in the post-crisis era has been met with uncommon circumstances in that central bank policies – including unprecedented purchases of over USD 12 trillion of sovereign debt and other assets – have contributed to historically low yields (Figure 1.3). For the first time in modern finance, sovereigns are being compensated by investors to issue debt: by year end 2016, USD 12 trillion in debt – 15% of the Barclays' Global Aggregate Bond Index – was trading at negative yields (PIMCO, 2018). In turn the combination of very low interest rates and historically low to negative bond yields have created conditions such that growing vulnerabilities from indebtedness may not be adequately priced by market participants that were indirectly competing with central banks to purchase debt instruments.

Moreover, the global reduction of yield for much of the post-crisis period has had a similar effect on the entire market – by design – to bring down yields across the risk curve (Figure 1.3), and to reduce the credit and equity risk premia. The policy motivation was to facilitate conditions that support ample financing for capital investment, business expansion, and economic growth. These factors may have contributed to the uptick in public trust in at least some OECD countries, as the public experienced renewed benefits from well-coordinated and effective stimulus measures.

Figure 1.3. Major central banks total balance sheet and interest rates, 2007-2018

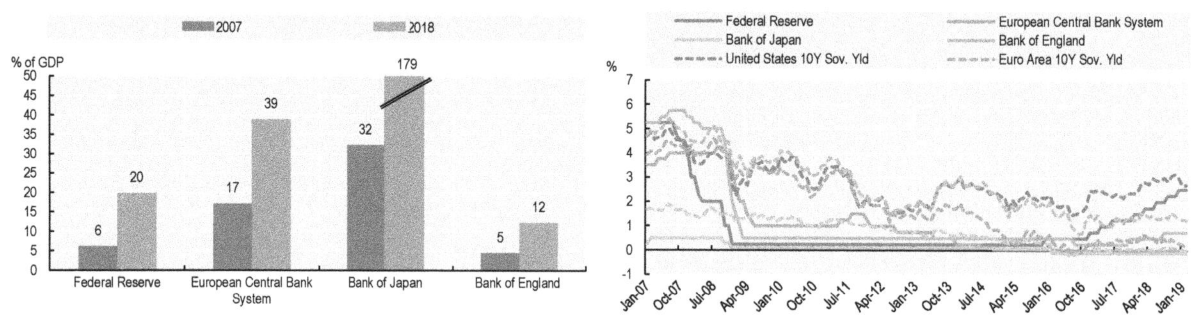

Source: Refinitiv, OECD calculations.

High levels of sovereign debt to GDP, while contributing to needed post-crisis fiscal stimulus in many countries, has in at least some OECD countries governments are not currently taking long-term actions that counteract the increases in debts (Beqiraj, et. al., 2018). This can complicate the path of debt sustainability in less benign rate and credit conditions. While certain countries have room to continue to provide fiscal stimulus in a low-rate environment, others may face more tenuous debt dynamics.[7]

These factors raise concerns about the impact of very accommodative monetary and fiscal policies on the level of debt, and the influence of exuberant pricing of market assets on the sustainability of current valuations and, in turn, the wealth effect. To the extent that abrupt changes in policy and underlying conditions contribute to sharp market repricing, it could have effects on the public's trust in the efficacy of post-crisis financial policies.

1.2.2. Corporate debt

Accommodative monetary policies and increasingly benign credit conditions were meant to create favourable financing conditions for corporate issuers, thereby allowing businesses to reinvest excess cash flows into productive businesses. However, these policies also incentivised businesses to take on additional corporate debt and restructure balance sheets to engineer higher returns to equity. As a result, corporate debt has grown 30% over the past decade to USD 70 trillion in 2018, rising from 81 to 92% of GDP in 2018 (Figure 1.4).

Figure 1.4. Non-Financial corporate outstanding debt for selected economies, 2000-2018

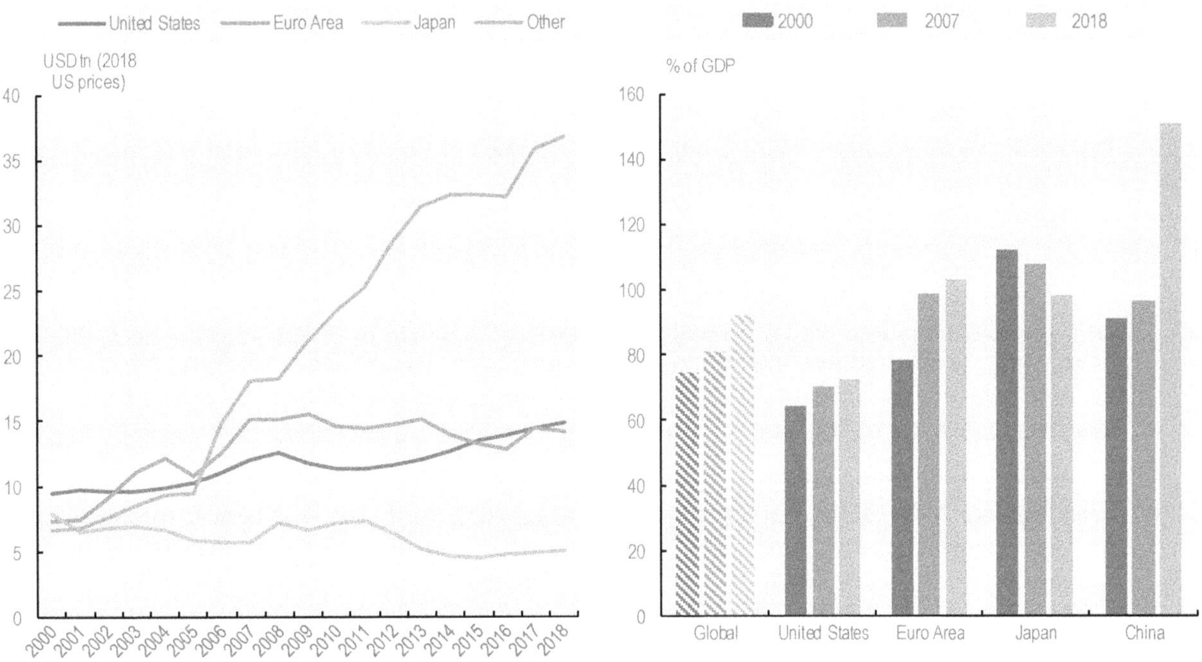

Note: The financial instruments covered comprise currency and deposits (which are mostly zero in the case of credit to the private non-financial sector), loans and debt securities. The sum of these three instruments is defined here as "core debt". Debt data for 63 countries are used in this chart. Outstanding amounts are presented in 2018 USD adjusted by US Consumer Price Index.
Source: Bank of International Settlements, Credit to the non-financial sector database, OECD calculations.

This growth has been accompanied by improved earnings and risk-adjusted returns on equity in many corporate sectors[8], in part due to lower debt financing costs that improve earnings per share. Certainly, solid returns to debt and equity from 2012 to 2018, and in turn improving corporate sector employment in many parts of OECD would be expected to restore an element of trust to the role of financial markets to contribute to inclusive economic growth.

Yet, a closer look indicates fragilities in the sustainability of debt, the use of debt proceeds, amid weak corporate productivity. The high level of corporate debt has occurred through very high issuance of corporate bonds and loans through market-based intermediation. During this period, corporate bond markets have more than doubled since 2007, rising to nearly USD 12 trillion, and USD 1.5 trillion of this amount was issued by speculative grade corporates (Çelik et al., 2019). Of the remaining, nearly USD 2.5 trillion of US corporate issuance is of BBB quality, which is prone to downgrade to non-investment grade rating amid deteriorating credit conditions, and may no longer be held by a portion of institutional investors. As well, the leveraged loan market (by which non-investment grade and highly leveraged corporates issue higher-yielding loans to investors) has more than doubled and by some estimates is more than USD 2.3 trillion in 2018 (Patalano and Roulet, 2019). Issuer leverage in the market, a sign of credit risk, has peaked such that deals with more that 6x debt to equity now represent a quarter of all issuance (Guggenheim Investments, 2018).

Box 1.1. Market integrity – quality of financial information

One key element of public trust in markets is the quality and relevance of financial information provided to market participants. Participants in financial markets rely on high-quality financial information of companies in order to make informed investment decisions and for asset managers to comply with fiduciary duties toward their clients. The trust in financial statements of corporate issuers is critical for the financial markets to interpret and respond to financial information in an efficient manner. This credibility is of the utmost importance when investor confidence is challenged by unforeseen market conditions and contagion.

Market integrity issues were brought to the forefront of concerns during the early 2000s, when Enron defaulted, and subsequent defaults of telecoms companies uncovered similarly faulty audits that contributed to hundreds of billions of dollars in investor losses through defaults and severe declines in telecoms stock valuations. The US Congress responded to the corporate corruption and fraud elements of the telecom meltdown by passing the Sarbanes-Oxley Act of 2002.

In certain jurisdictions, concerns over audit quality and fee structure are again under consideration. In 2018, the UK Competition and Markets Authority was called to review the UK financial reporting authority's conduct related to the review of the Big Four Accounting firms. In late 2018, the UK Competition and Markets Authority issued several recommendations to address these concerns by, among other issues, improving auditor independence, recommending an operational split between the Big Four's audit and non-audit businesses, to ensure maximum focus on audit quality.

Also, in 2017, the monitoring group comprising IOSCO, FSB, et. al., released a consultation paper, "Strengthening the Governance and Oversight of the International Audit-Related Standard-Setting Boards in the Public Interest", that highlights concerns about the current international auditing and ethics standard-setting model. The consultation paper notes that there may be an adverse effect on stakeholder confidence in the standards as a result of a perception of undue influence on the standard-setting process by the accounting and auditing professions, through their funding and direct staffing of standard-setting boards. The monitoring group has received feedback from the public consultation of its paper, which it summarised publicly, and IFAC has put forth viewpoints based on an independent review of the responses to the monitoring group's consultation. The Monitoring Group has the benefit of this feedback and IFAC is reviewing identified operational areas with IAASB and IESBA leadership and other stakeholders to determine the actions they would agree can be taken now to improve the efficiency and effectiveness of the operations of the two boards in the public interest.

The issuance reflects a deepening of capital markets in many countries, particularly those that are facilitating a shift away from bank-dominated finance. However, high-yield bond and leveraged loan yields, which peaked at 22% and 16% respectively during the crisis, have fallen to below 5% amid investors' reach for yield. Monetary policy, by design, indirectly supported the compression of corporate bond spreads in North America and Asia, and also directly did so in the euro area following the ECB's corporate bond purchasing programme.

To what extent do these market risks outweigh the benefit of additional low-cost financing to corporates for capital investment? During this period, many corporations engaged aggressively to boost returns to equity holders through share buybacks and dividends rather than in capital expenditures (OECD, 2015),which may have contributed to tepid corporate sector growth despite the public-sector stimulus.

Moreover, there is ample evidence that growth of corporate productivity in many OECD countries slowed during this period until 2017, due to sluggish capital investment to GDP relative to its contribution in the prior recovery in the 2000s (OECD, 2015); OECD, 2018a). These observations suggest that while monetary policy was successful in propping up asset prices to allow for cheaper financing and investor wealth effect, it did not contribute fundamentally to fostering capex-driven growth and greater productivity, which are important elements of medium-term debt sustainability.[9]

1.2.3. Bank contingent-convertible bonds

In addition to corporate bonds, the market for bank contingent convertible or "CoCo" bonds experienced notable growth. These bonds were permitted by regulators in the post-crisis period to help banks raise debt that could be converted to equity in the event banks experience losses that erode regulatory capital buffers. The purpose of the convertible debt is to help ensure that banks considered too big to fail do not impose losses to taxpayers. In addition, the explicit guidance by authorities to limit inter-bank holding of loss-absorbing debt helps ensure that the contingent losses would be widely distributed across market participants to limit concentrations of loss in systemically-important entities. At the same time, the bail-in regimes and conversion of loss-absorbing capital creates uncertainty which could, under some circumstances, result in market contagion as losses are imposed on institutional and retail holders.

The market for contingent convertible bonds has risen substantially, as annual issuance has risen from under USD 25 billion in 2008 to an average of USD 150 billion of issuance since 2014, contributing to an approximated outstanding of greater than USD 500 billion (Figure 1.5).[10] European banks and, more recently, Chinese banks have issued most heavily into the market.

Initially, CoCo bonds faced several challenges in generating investor demand. First, the convertible nature of the bonds complicates valuation of their bond and equity-like structures. Second, the contingent element of the bonds depends in part on the regulatory treatment, and the bonds may be required to convert to equity due to banks' failure to pass supervisory stress tests, rather than actual losses. Due to these features, the bonds are generally considered to have low liquidity, and have experienced wide price fluctuations during periods of market stress, in comparison to non-convertible bonds of corporates and banks. To this end, there is evidence of recent contagion in the European CoCo bond market, which has exceeded USD 150 billion, as application of bail-in has given rise to uncertainty over the consistency of treatment (Bologna et al., 2018).

Figure 1.5. Bank's convertible bond issuance and blended-spread, 2001-2019

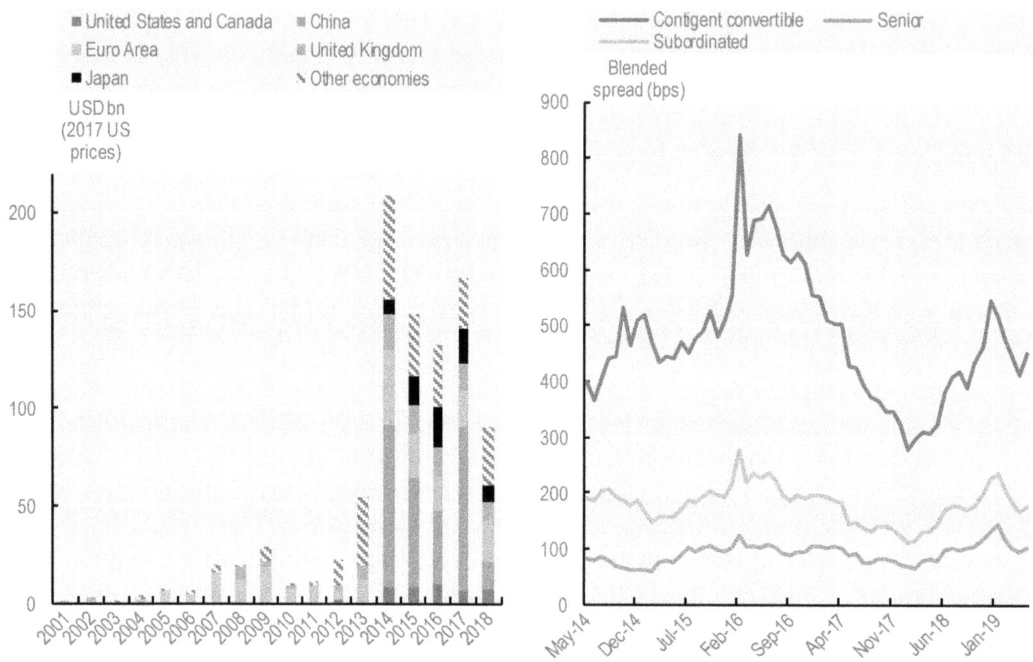

Note: Only contingent convertible bonds issued by banks are included in the statistics (i.e., contingent convertible (write-down) and contingent convertible (conversion)). Issuance amounts are presented in 2017 USD adjusted by US Consumer Price Index. Three Bloomberg Barclays global bond banking indices are shown depending on the type of underlying bond, i.e. contingent convertible, senior or subordinated. Blended spread represents the difference between bond index yield versus US Treasuries.
Source: Refinitiv, OECD calculations.

The investor base of these forms of loss-absorbing bank capital has shifted from primarily long-term institutional investors to a greater retail base (Boermans and Wijnbergen, 2017). In particular open-ended investment funds have substantially increased holdings of CoCo debt. Recent evidence suggests that retail investment funds are now the largest holders of bank CoCo bonds, either as funds targeting higher-yielding bank exposures, or as investments within broad fund categories, whereas European household direct exposure to CoCos has declined sharply. Moreover, the primary investors in European funds with CoCo exposure are non-residents, which suggests they may be less knowledgeable of European banking conditions and regulatory treatment.

The key driver of the growing demand is that, amid investors' reach for yield, CoCo bond yields are well above 5%, which is higher than most other fixed-income products in Europe. In this regard, anecdotal evidence suggests that a number of fixed income funds are allowed to hold up to certain portion of such bonds, such as a 10% limit. Therefore, investors may be less aware of the specific CoCo exposure in their fixed-income portfolios.

In sum, while the reach for yield and strong performance of these bonds may have contributed to a growing sense of investor confidence in the CoCos as an asset class, the untested nature of the bail-in regimes in different parts of the world could eventually give rise to unexpected outcomes that could sharply alter perception of risks of these products.

1.2.4. Debt outlook and implications for Trust

The outlook for debt markets is highly dependent on economic, credit and market conditions. Following years of very low rates and highly liquid primary market conditions, a sharp change in rates and repricing of market and credit risks would have substantial effects on market valuations and liquidity. In 2019, forecasts by the OECD indicate that growth among OECD countries is slowing after several years of synchronous growth. In addition, political uncertainty (e.g. political events such as Brexit) and trade tensions have contributed to eroding business confidence (OECD, 2019a). While the eventual normalisation of central bank rates would be expected to increase yields and financing costs, other factors – such as geopolitical uncertainties, a deterioration of credit conditions, and lack of competitiveness -- could give rise to much higher financing costs and spillovers to related markets, which would increase the liquidity risk premia. To the extent that buoyant markets and historically benign financing conditions contributed to the improved trust in finance in recent years, an abrupt reversal of these conditions due to economic or political factors could in turn erode public trust in these markets.

Sovereign debt outlook and implications

In light of growing risks, many sovereign borrowers have taken the opportunity in this low-rate environment to extend their maturity schedule to reduce the amount of debt needing to be refinanced over the next several years (OECD, 2019b). Nevertheless, the amount of near-term maturing debt is relatively high for a number of OECD countries, on average approximately 40% of total debt outstanding (Figure 1.6).

Figure 1.6. Cumulative percentage of sovereign debt maturing in the next 12, 24 and 36 months, 2019-2021

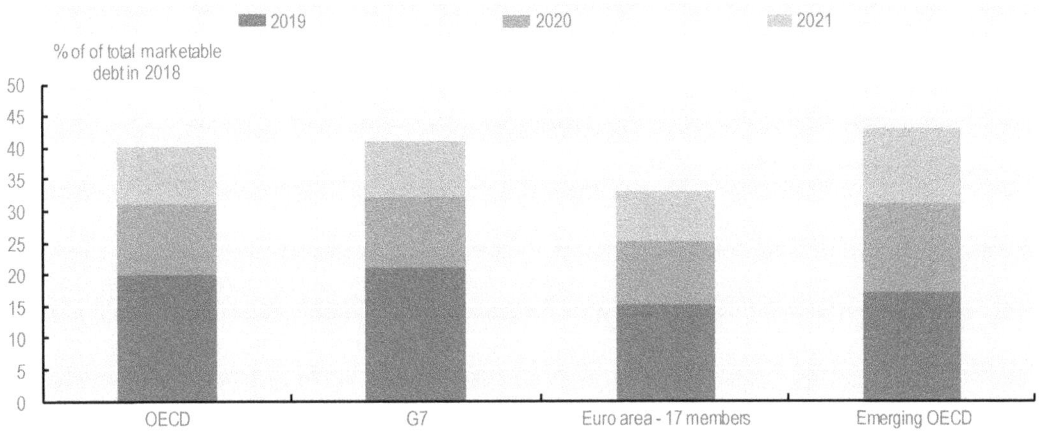

Note: Cumulative percentage of debt maturing in the next 12, 24 and 36 months (i.e. in 2019, 2020 and 2021), as a percentage of total marketable debt stock (without cash) in 2018. Values of principal payments and marketable debt have been aggregated into a single currency by using fixed exchange rates, as of 1st December 2009, for all years. The Emerging OECD group is defined as Chile, Hungary, Mexico, Poland and Turkey.
Source: 2018 Survey on Central Government Marketable Debt and Borrowing; OECD Economic Outlook No. 104; Refinitiv, national authorities' websites and OECD calculations.

In a rising rate environment, the cost of new debt issuance will depend upon funding needs, the rate differential relative to debt maturing and the extent to which the debt was hedged by debt agencies. For a number of countries, a rollover of one-third of debt at even 200bps higher debt yields would stretch fiscal deficits due to higher interest costs.[11] Rising debt vulnerability concerns in some countries could push credit risk premia on sovereign debt higher and trigger collateral downgrades, further contributing to market stress (Nickel and Tudyka, 2013); Taylor, 2018). While idiosyncratic defaults may impact investor confidence, they may not necessarily erode public trust in the debt markets unless such defaults expose faultlines that suggest widespread flaws in market behaviours and oversight that permitted a pervasive underassessment of risk. Particularly if the rising risk aversion is in response to policy decisions that are perceived to heighten market uncertainty, authorities' responses could have consequences for public trust. The extent to which public trust might be eroded would at least partly depend upon the extent to which unanticipated losses are distributed across market participants, and the extent to which any costs are indirectly socialised, such as from subsidising losses through bail-outs, or cutting the social safety net.

Corporate debt outlook and implications

Corporate debt issuers that are highly levered would experience similar dynamics. Given elevated corporate debt to GDP and operating cash flows in many countries (Figure 1.7), the combination of rising rates and slower growth would erode the debt sustainability of a growing portion of leveraged issuers, and could contribute to a considerable rise in ratings downgrades and defaults. Such pressures and ratings movements, in turn, would cause investors to demand a higher credit risk premia, exacerbating debt financing costs.

Figure 1.7. Non-financial companies' debt to EBITDA ratio for selected economies, 2002-2018

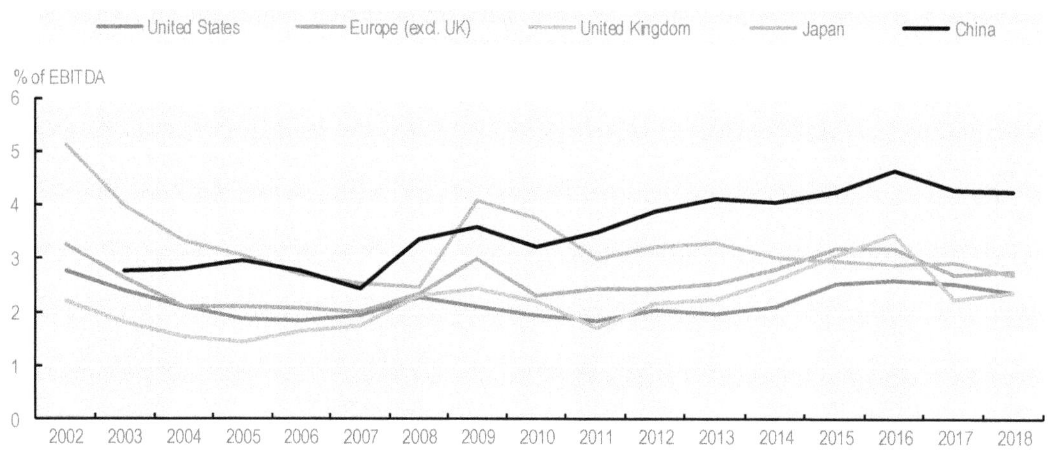

Note: EBITDA represents income before interest, taxes, depreciation and amortisation. Total debt includes loans and short and long-term bonds. Financials companies listed in S&P 500, STOXX 600 and Thomson Reuters Japan and China equity indices are excluded. Annual consolidated financial statements are collected on an annual basis, at the firm level and in current USD. The current primary source of this information is Refinitiv and some data are extracted from Bloomberg. All variables are trimmed at the 1st and 99th percentile levels to reduce the effect of outliers.
Source: Refinitiv, OECD calculations.

This is particularly the case in advanced economy markets where leveraged lending is sizeable, such as the United States and the United Kingdom. Unlike high yield debt, which is mostly fixed-rate, leverage loans are floating rate, which means that debt costs rise both due to rising interest rates that cause loan payments to reset, as well as the credit risk premia. Moreover, there are concerns that the prominence of cov-lite loans will result in much higher losses when issuers default, which would contribute to a more substantial repricing of risk relative to the financial crisis (Federal Reserve, 2019).

Rising corporate defaults and losses would erode the resilience of debtholders, including banks, finance companies, asset managers, insurance and pension funds. Depending on their risk management frameworks, these institutions would face pressures to reduce credit exposures through costly hedging or portfolio rebalancing to sell assets, which would further contribute to market liquidity costs. Also, given the substantial increase of BBB debt in the market, many institutions that have limits on non-investment grade debt would need to sell or hedge BBB debt in the event of downgrades to ratings below investment grade (Celik et al., 2019).

A moderate increase in yields, from credit spread widening and/or precautionary rate increases, could have significant impact on debt sustainability, particularly in large emerging market economies. A study by McKinsey Global Institute illustrates the consequences: in a simulation of a 200-basis-point rise in rates, the share of bonds at higher risk of default in Brazil, China, and India could rise to 30 to 40 percent. The share of bonds at higher risk of default in Brazil and India might rise to roughly 30% of total corporate bonds outstanding. China's share of corporate bonds at higher risk of default could rise to over 40 percent from 2017 levels. Should these outcomes occur, they will weigh heavily on EME banking sector asset quality, and banks' ability to intermediate credit to businesses and households (McKinsey, 2018b).

Bank CoCos outlook and implications

Bank CoCo bonds are now largely in the hands of retail and some institutional investors such as pension funds and insurers. While these binds have delivered high yields in a low rate environment, their performance during market stress and deteriorating bank asset quality, and the extent of cross-border contagion to non-European investors, will have implications for investor trust in asset class.

For example, in Europe the regulatory authorities have powers to direct the conversion of CoCos to equity pursuant to the Bank Recovery and Resolution Directive (BRRD), which can then impose losses on holders. Under the BRRD framework, the national resolution authorities may also exclude specific liabilities from the application of the bail-in if there is a risk of widespread contagion. As these criteria can be broadly interpreted, the process and outcome on the CoCo investors' situation is unpredictable (Philippon and Salo, 2017).

Moreover, a portion of banks across OECD countries will continue to need to raise total loss-absorbing capital to meet regulatory requirements. Should the triggering of bail-in conversions of CoCos result in greater scrutiny of the bail-in mechanisms and widespread risk aversion due to heightened uncertainty, then trust in regulatory and market authorities regarding the fairness of loss distribution (e.g. to retail investors) may erode.

Implication for trust of rising debt

Thus, a decade after excessive debt in the housing market contributed to the financial crisis, widespread stress in the sovereign, corporate credit, and bank CoCo markets could draw public scrutiny to the effectiveness of post-crisis reforms. Widespread losses on debt could give rise to a loss of investor trust in the post-crisis policies that promoted portfolio rebalancing and engineered a market-wide reach for yield. These effects could be particularly detrimental to trust in intermediaries, such as public pension funds and defined-contribution funds, as negative impacts to post-retirement benefits or increases in mandatory contributions could raise societal concerns about the long-term viability of existing pension frameworks.[12]

Moreover, should much tighter financial conditions occur, it could lead to higher defaults of public and private companies, which would eventually have an impact on employment, and could dampen credit intermediation to SMEs more extensively, thereby slowing economic growth. Should this occur, at least some countries might be faced with rising fiscal costs and conditions that pin central bank policies toward the lower bound.

1.3. The rise of market-based finance

A second phenomenon in financial markets in the period since the Global Financial Crisis is the continued rise of non-bank financial intermediation and, in particular, market-based finance. Market-based finance can be described as financial intermediation by financial institutions, vehicles, and products that finance themselves from the markets rather than banks or other forms of direct institutional lending.

Investors may be attracted to market-based finance due to opportunity for higher risk-adjusted returns than bank deposits, and greater diversification of risk. Such intermediation, appropriately conducted, provides a valuable alternative to bank funding that supports real economic activity. Therefore, the investing public's trust in the efficiency and effectiveness of market-based finance to deliver superior risk adjusted returns, and the integrity and transparency of markets and traded products is particularly important. Moreover, public trust extends to faith that the oversight authorities are able to ensure that imbalances and excesses do not lead to financial stability risks that eventually cause widespread and deep losses.

Public trust is critical to the growth and stability of market-based finance because, unlike banks, these forms of intermediation do not benefit from established access to financial safety nets, such as deposit guarantees or central bank backstops, or from the scrutiny of bank supervision. Thus, where maturity and liquidity mismatches exist, they can become susceptible to runs. This phenomenon led to the amplification of risk within and across markets during the financial crisis, and contributed to a sharp erosion of market confidence. As the contagion spread back to the banking system and impeded the provision of credit to the real economy, public trust in the financial system deteriorated.

1.3.1. The growth of investment funds and structured products

During the post crisis era, market-based financial systems stabilised as various forms of the so-called "toxic" products, such as subprime collateralised debt obligations (CDOs), declined. At the same time, other forms of market-based finance have grown and appear to have gained an element of trust. In particular, very strong growth of forms of asset management vehicles have occurred in part due to demand for transparency and efficient, loss-cost diversification of risk, which has contributed to passive investing through index funds and exchange traded funds (ETFs).

The growth of investment funds to intermediate credit

In the decade since the crisis, investors' reach for yield in a low-rate environment has contributed to the growth of a range of open-ended investment funds and exchange-traded investment funds that provide higher returns and risks than traditional money market funds. Innovations in the asset management industry, including passive funds and liquid alternatives, have contributed to a rise in open-ended investment funds' assets under management to USD 50 trillion (Figure 1.8). The growth has brought benefits in terms of financial inclusion and greater access to capital from lower-rated corporates and Emerging Market issuers, at competitive financing rates.

Figure 1.8. Global growth of open-end investment funds, 2008-2017

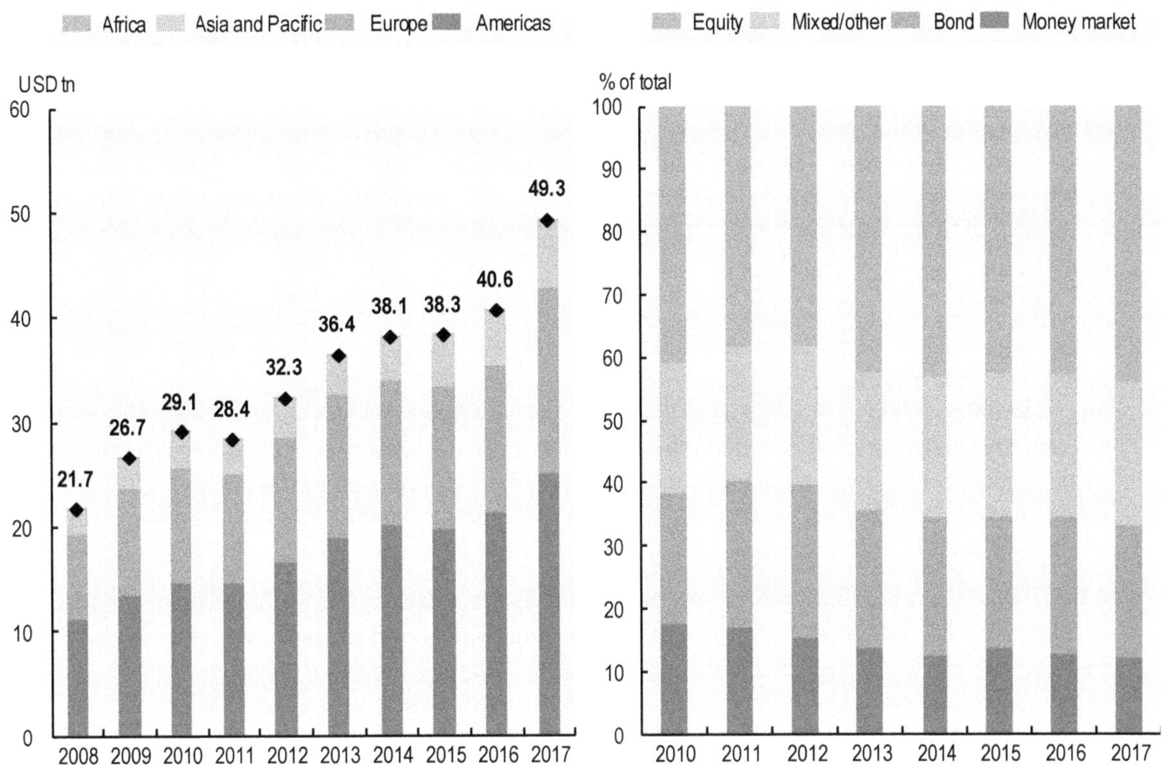

Note: Regulated open-end funds include mutual, institutional and exchange-traded funds.
Source: Investment Company Institute, International Investment Fund Association.

Also, the growth of low-cost, highly diversified exchange-traded funds (ETFs) has contributed to improved financial deepening, and greater ability for institutional and retail investors to diversify holdings across asset classes and geographies. Moreover, the proliferation of funds has increased investor choice; greater, more consistent and more transparent financial information; and greater ability to tailor investments to particular industries or strategies. To this end, the rise of sustainable investment funds (including environmental, social and governance ESG investing) illustrates growing investor interest in financial products that enhance risk assessment and better aligned with societal values to seek long-term value. That investors are increasingly utilising this diversity of investment products, and at much lower costs, may suggest greater trust in the functioning, transparency and liquidity of the product adaptations.

One positive aspect of credit intermediation through asset managers is that the asset management entities themselves are generally considered resilient. Because they are not the asset owners and the funds are generally not leveraged (as constrained by regulation), these funds do not share the features of banks or broker dealers that are exposed to high leverage from short term liabilities, and thus default risk.

Nevertheless, investment funds do have certain features that might amplify market stress. As open-ended investment funds provide daily liquidity to investors through on-demand redemptions of fund shares, investors expect to be able to exit funds at short notice with little impact to prevailing market prices. While this may be true for individual trades, such funds may be subject to investor runs when risk aversion suddenly rises and heightened redemptions of funds occurs.[13] In addition, features of at least some funds contribute to a first-mover advantage, whereby redeeming investors do not bear the full cost of redemptions, and instead these costs are borne by remaining unit holders.

These features could become problematic in open-ended funds that invest in less liquid assets, or assets that are more likely to experience sharp decreases in liquidity during periods of market stress. The rise of funds holding high-yield corporate bonds, bank CoCo bonds, emerging market bonds, and leveraged loans have contributed to the rise of debt in advanced and emerging market economies. Should credit conditions deteriorate, the eroding quality of debt held by certain funds could prove to be the driver of outflows on falling returns.

Thus, heavy redemptions in bond funds that do not effectively manage liquidity risk could, under extreme circumstances, force selling of assets that exacerbates downward price movements and asset price contagion across related markets. While such episodes are uncommon, there are concerns that greater levels of open-ended funds, a decline in broker-dealer capacity to engage in fixed-income market making, and rich market valuations have made market liquidity more fragile. Thus, fixed-income market stress in a rising rate environment amid deteriorating credit conditions could be more consequential in the future.

Also, ETFs that trade in less liquid markets, such as corporate and emerging market bonds, or loans, could also contribute to spillovers in the underlying markets under periods of market stress. ETF mechanisms utilise selected market participants to serve as "authorised participants" to create and redeem ETF shares when the underlying assets deviate from the share price. However, these APs are under no obligation to engage in this market arbitrage to align the prices. During some prior periods of stress, the value of shares of at least some ETF deviated substantially from the value of underlying assets for brief intervals, suggesting that authorised participants did not sufficiently engage in voluntary arbitrage that would ensure market efficiency. While ETFs are generally perceived as having equity-like liquidity, such liquidity may prove illusory for some funds that can only sell assets at a significant discount in times of stress (Central Bank of Ireland, 2017).

As the growth of asset management has resulted in a much larger amount of debt, (including high yield corporate debt, EM debt, and leveraged loans) in funds' assets under management, investor trust in the orderly functioning of the funds during periods of stress in fixed income markets could be tested.

Structured products

One of the most notable developments in non-bank financial intermediation in the decade prior to the crisis was the sharp rise of structured products that pooled various credit exposures (such as mortgages, trade receivables, commercial real estate, and leveraged loans), and issued units or tranches of liabilities that catered to investors' demand for particular risk exposures. In this manner, financial engineering was able to transform and market risks and returns in an array of offerings, and distribute them outside of the banking system to investors seeking higher returns.

Some forms of these innovations experienced unexpected and heavy losses during the financial crisis. Shadow banking products such as subprime CDOs, credit arbitrage asset backed commercial paper vehicles (ABCP), and structured investment funds (SIVs), were a key factor in the loss of public trust, because they contributed not only to investor losses but also to the demise of a number of institutions and the need for public sector intervention that put taxpayer resources at risk.[14]

With the demise of these riskier forms of structured products, arguably less opaque forms have grown in the aftermath of the crisis. One of the structures that was relatively resilient during the crisis was the collateralised loan obligation (CLO), which benefited from covenant-based protections in leveraged loans. Their growth illustrates the revival of the securitisation markets in the United States and Europe. While they provide benefits to investors looking for diversified higher yielding risks, there are potential risks associated with both the nature of credit risk, and the potential for the structures to perform badly.

CLOs are structured vehicles that purchase and manage portfolios of leveraged loans, and sell tranches of these portfolios with a range of ratings (AAA senior tranches through mezzanine B tranches, and equity) to provide tailored products to meet the risk and return demand of a range of institutional investors.[15] This tailoring allows CLOs to redistribute the high yields on risky leveraged loans (non-investment grade, by definition) and through tranching offer yields that are above similarly rated corporate debt. CLO managers earn a fee for managing the portfolio and where they hold equity, also receive returns on their investment through superior credit risk management.

CLO issuance and outstanding fell sharply after the financial crisis due to investor concerns over structured credit products, and the extreme volatility of CLO tranche spreads during the crisis. However, with the stabilisation of the leveraged loan markets resulting from improved credit conditions in the US and Europe, CLOs again became a popular investment vehicle due largely to the search for yields among institutional investors in an increasingly low yield environment. CLOs have grown to over USD 600 billion in the United States, and now own nearly 60% of the leveraged loan market (Figure 1.9).

A particular concern is that the underwriting standards of underlying leveraged loans has deteriorated. While bank loans include covenants to help lenders reduce borrowers actions that can increase financial risks, leveraged loan issuers have increasingly reduced covenant protections, and in return offer investors additional yield. While this has benefits during benign credit conditions, it can expose investors to higher losses when credit conditions deteriorate. Industry participants and regulators raised concerns when covenant light ("cov-lite") loans grew to 35% of leveraged loan issuance by 2007; cov-lites were over 80% of issuance in 2017 (S&P Ratings, 2018). As such, rating agencies and market analysts are raising concern over the potential for significant losses during the next credit downturn.

CLO holdings are dispersed widely across institutional investors. While institutional investors traditionally held triple-A tranches of the CLOs, the reach for yield has incentivised insurers, pension funds, and asset managers to demand lower rated A and BBB tranches, which would perform considerably worse than similarly-rated corporate bonds during deteriorating economic and credit conditions.[16] Moreover, due to their illiquidity, the mark-to-market volatility on tranche spreads are significantly higher than comparable corporate bond prices during periods of market turbulence.

Figure 1.9. Leveraged loans and US CLOs, 1998-2018

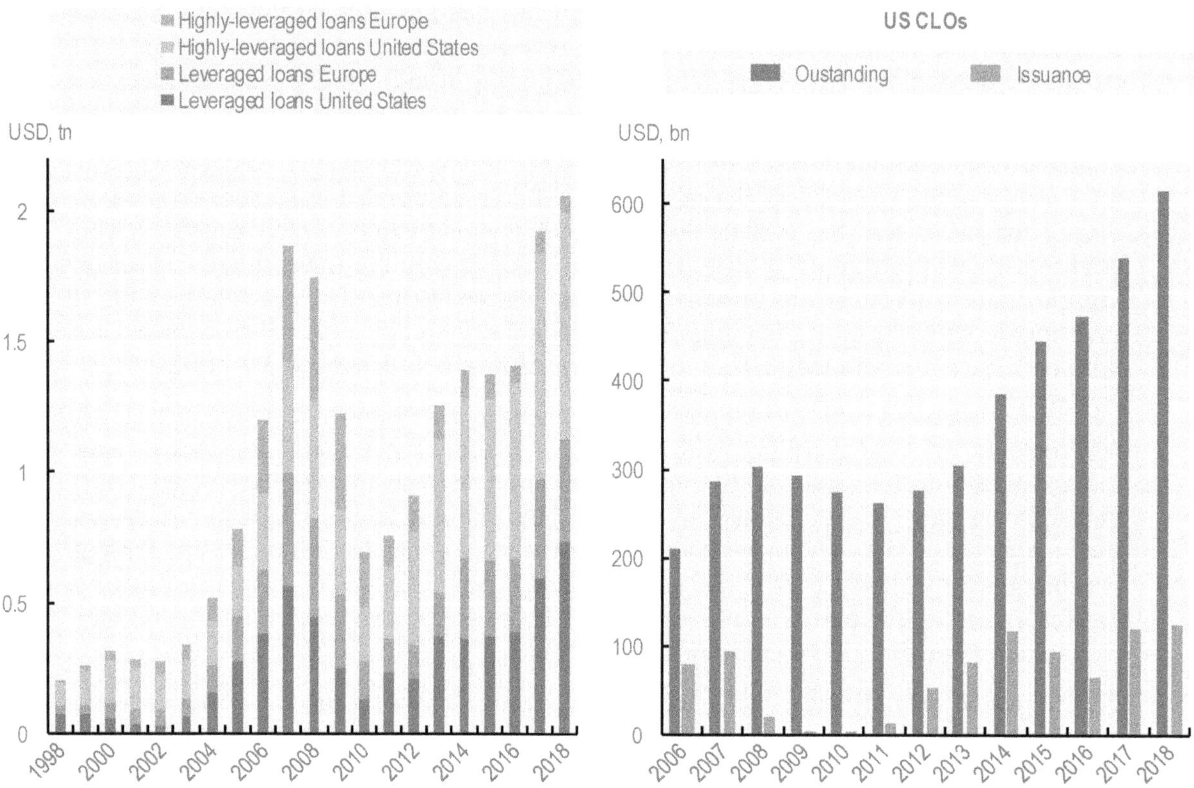

Note: Data show in this figure are derived from leveraged and highly leveraged loan deals in the United States and Europe from twelve economic sectors over the period 1990-2018. Outstanding amount is calculated based on loan issuance but excludes the value of drawn and undrawn revolving credit facilities. Linear amortisation schedule is postulated for term loans A and other amortising loans (i.e., mortgages, equipment, construction, commercial loans). All other terms loans are not amortised as they are repayable at maturity. To account for loan re-financing, a 40% early repayment ratio is used. Financial companies are excluded from the sample.
Source: Refinitiv, SIFMA, OECD calculations.

1.3.2. Market-based finance outlook: consequences of a repricing of debt on liquidity

Investment funds

The growth of investment funds has been beneficial with respect to product choice, diversification, dramatically lower costs, and increasing transparency of performance and risks. In this manner, it has brought the benefit of stable post-crisis returns to a wider span of the investing community, who perceive that the liquidity provision from open-ended funds and ETFs allow for rapid exit of markets should market sentiment sour. Notwithstanding these important benefits, the significant growth of credit in open-ended funds raises concerns about continued performance during a period of deteriorating credit conditions, and in light of structural features of open-ended funds that may make them susceptible to run-risk and herding (where multiple funds and other investors' selling reinforces collective selling behaviours).

It is important to note that the international policy debate over the extent of run-risk, fund herding, and contagion has benefited from a wide range of research on the behaviours of funds, institutional investors, and fixed-income market liquidity. Results about the extent of such behaviour in past crisis episodes are mixed, and there is ample evidence that funds contributed to restore market liquidity in at least some episodes of stress, as market prices deviated significantly from what participants considered to be fair or intrinsic asset value.

Nonetheless, a body of research suggests that funds, while not the cause of market runs, could contribute in some scenarios to runs in less liquid markets due to first-mover advantage, herding, and negative feedback dynamics where investors respond to an initial round of losses by selling additional fund shares, causing forced asset sales (Cetorelli et al., 2016). Moreover, there is some evidence that during periods of market stress, such funds would sell even more assets than needed to meet redemptions in an effort to improve cash or liquid asset buffers (Morris and Shin, 2017). A simulation of corporate bond markets by the Bank of England suggests that a severe but plausible set of assumptions regarding market participant behaviours, redemptions from open-ended investment funds can result in material increases in spreads in the European corporate bond market. In the extreme, this could lead to dislocations in corporate bond markets (Baranova et al., 2017).

Thus, potential liquidity risks from open-ended funds and ETFs, among other instruments, could contribute to unexpected losses for investors who were not invested in these products during a prior credit downturn, and could also contribute to greater spillovers in underlying markets. Products such as leveraged loan or bank CoCo ETFs, while a small part of the market, may be sensitive to deteriorating credit conditions, and sharp declines in their market values could contribute to reduced confidence in the ability of investors to exit these products on demand.

To the extent these events occur, they could erode the fragile restoration of trust since the financial crisis. Such erosion could have a financial impact, through higher costs of equity and debt financing, reduced market access of higher-risk borrowers, fragile market liquidity and higher cost of trading in normal and stressed market conditions. In turn, these costs would tighten financial conditions, and the efficiency losses would be borne by government, corporate and household borrowers, affecting economic growth.

CLOs

The outlook for the CLO market, and its potential for loss during deteriorating credit conditions, merits a review of myriad regulatory efforts to address misalignments of risk in leveraged loan and CLO structures.

In light of growing risks in the leveraged loan markets, US authorities issued leveraged loan guidance to regulated banks and non-bank subsidiaries of bank holding companies to limit the amount of leverage in syndicated deals. There is evidence that the guidance helped reduce the riskiness of leveraged loans syndicated by banks; however, the overall market continued to grow due to increased regulatory arbitrage by non-bank syndicators (Kim et al., 2016).

In 2014, US and European regulators and banking authorities adopted credit risk retention rules for securitisations, which sought to align the incentives of originators with tranche investors, to minimise morale hazard. The rules served to "keep skin in the game" by ensuring that securitisers held a portion of equity in the CLO, to align their incentive to minimise losses for the entire CLO structure (Federal Reserve, 2014). The CLO market outpaced its pre-crisis peak as private equity and other institutional investors contributed equity to this market, which raises questions as to the effect of the regulation on the securitisation process.

Nevertheless, this regulation was considered onerous by the industry, which raised concerns that it could hamper the viability of the CLO market. In early 2018, a US Court of Appeals exempted managers of open-market CLOs from the risk retention rule.[17] Consequently, CLO securitisers' ability to distribute risk may introduce the potential for misaligned incentives, when the CLO sponsors' equity is no longer at risk.

In 2018, CLO managers have begun to distribute the equity tranches to other investors, including to retail investors through open-ended funds. While some investor communications claim that the equity has performed well during the cycle, the structures have not experienced a credit downturn amid rising interest rates, which imposed severe losses on CLO equity during the financial crisis. Moreover, CLO equity is highly illiquid and has higher risk characteristics than the underlying leverage loans themselves. From a policy perspective, the growth of this practice could invite scrutiny to the adequacy of investor protection and suitability.

From a markets perspective, growing losses in CLOs could have several consequences. First, it could transmit losses to CLO subordinated tranche holders, trigger higher spreads on senior tranches, and impose losses on banks, insurers and asset managers. Also, growing losses could curtail CLO demand for leveraged loans, which could contribute to much higher financing costs for highly leveraged companies, thereby elevating defaults and restructuring within the industry. This spillover to the real economy might contribute to a broader decline in credit conditions, whereby rising underwriting standards and risk aversion further tighten financial conditions for corporate financing.

Implications for trust of rising market-based finance

In the post-crisis era, the international community of financial stability and regulatory authorities has make concerted efforts to address the riskiest forms of non-bank financial intermediation through a suite of financial policy measures.

However, should evolving risks in parts of market-base finance expose new faultiness that could have financial stability implications, it could erode public trust in the efficacy and completeness of post-crisis financial reforms. In particular, unexpectedly high leveraged loan and CLO losses that impact investment funds and pensions, respectively, which would be felt more directly by the investing public. This could erode public trust in the post-crisis policy response to the high-yield and securitisation markets, as well as in bodies who concluded that the most concerning shadow banking risks had largely been addressed (FSB, 2017b).

As well, higher losses in and amplification of risks from funds, should they occur, may raise broader concerns about the resilience of fixed-income market liquidity, and trust in products that have substituted prudent credit risk assessment for market liquidity.

1.4. Financial innovations

One of the most prominent developments in finance in the post-crisis period has been the development and adoption of financial technologies, or "Fintech". These technologies are broadly associated with either the use of distributed ledger (blockchain) technologies, or the use of advanced computing in finance, such as through the application of artificial intelligence combined with highly sophisticated analytics and computer power. Also, the use of blockchain has supported the development of crypto-assets, which are digital asset that function to varying degrees as a medium of exchange and that use strong cryptography to secure financial transactions. Application of these technologies has led to the proliferation of high-frequency and algorithmic trading in financial markets, and also the use of forms of crypto-assets for more efficient payments, trading and investments.

The growing use of distributed ledger technology has implications for the speed, efficiency, cross-border reach, and potentially the security of financial transactions (OECD, 2018b). As well, the availability and value of crypto-assets have growth exponentially in recent years, as investors seek alternative and decentralised ways to create market value and transact in a highly-secured and immutable manner.

The rapid growth of these financial innovations has benefited from a certain level of investor and financial consumer trust in the benefits of digitalisation in finance. In this regard, an important element of this trust is the extent to which market participants and consumers have positive engagement with various financial technologies that improve speed and cost efficiencies, inclusion through access to financial services, and improved data security. However, these rapidly growing technologies have been mostly untested during periods of sharp downturn and volatility, or major cyber events. Notwithstanding the promise of these technologies, major incidents that involve loss, traditional fraud, cyber theft, and malfunctioning could quickly undermine the public's current engagement, and may raise concerns about the further proliferation of the use of such technology in the financial system. As with any innovations, the outcomes of a changing competitive landscape and opportunities for regulatory arbitrage could have unintended consequences that give rise to distrust.

This section further considers the developments related to several key aspects of the financial markets, including algorithmic and high-frequency trading, and the growth of crypto-assets. It assesses the growth and impact of these technologies over the past decade, and then considers the outlook, including risks and spillovers that could contribute to an erosion of investor and public trust.

1.4.1. Growth of trading electronification and crypto-assets

Algorithmic and high-frequency trading

Algorithmic and high-frequency trading refers to forms of electronification of market trading that rely on computer algorithms to execute order strategies, and the use of substantial technological power to execute trades very quickly, thereby gaining an advantage over traditional traders. Firms pursuing HFT strategies tend to generate a large number of orders, hold open positions for very short periods and cancel a large share of orders that they generate, which is only possible to execute effectively in markets that have sufficient liquid (BIS, 2016). This speed and agility has benefits in that it allows for operational and cost efficiencies, and can facilitate the absorption of new financial information into market prices.

Moreover, algorithmic high-frequency trading has become a much larger part of equity, FX, and increasingly fixed income markets, and also has grown considerably in the trading and market-making of ETFs. These technologies has lowered the cost and increased the speed of transactions, and are credited with providing additional liquidity to certain markets during normal market conditions.[18]

However, some strategies appear to have reduced liquidity and exacerbated flash crashes that have occurred with growing frequency over the past several years (Table 1.1). While these limited flash crashes have not led to broader market contagion, such incidents draw attention to questions about the resilience of market functioning. More turbulent outcomes that destabilise markets and contribute to widespread losses could challenge public perceptions with respect to the costs and benefits of algorithmic and high-frequency trading.

Table 1.1. Market flash crashes in selected economies, 2010-2019

Country	Market	Year
United States	S&P (equity)	2010
United States	Nasdaq (equity)	2013
United States	Treasury	2014
United States	NYSE (equity)	2015
United Kingdom	British Pound	2016
United States	Dow Jones (equity)	2018
Japan	Yen	2019

Source: OECD staff examples of large flash crash events, for illustrative purposes.

These types of trading occur both in established broker dealers and independent principal trading firms (PTFs), which have grown substantially in the post-crisis era. Such firms are distinct from broker-dealers in that they are not driven by client relationships and client driven orders, and do not need large balance sheet capacity to make markets. As such, their balance sheets are small, and they are (mostly) not subject to strict capital requirements.

Algo-HFT participants are now more prevalent in trading in equities and currencies, but are growing in bond trading. Also, PTFs are also becoming more prevalent market-makers and authorised participants for ETFs. Thus, they are not just relied upon for efficiency and speed, but as an increasingly central component of the liquidity provision of numerous financial products.

Of key concern to investors and policy makers is that there are a growing number of incidents of "flash crashes," in which these types of trading firms and algorithmic strategies appear to contribute to extreme market volatility. A prominent flash crash in equity markets occurred in May 2010, when the Dow Jones Industrial Average experienced its largest ever intraday point decline of 9%. An assessment of the causes of the flash crash by public and academic researchers found that while HFT did not cause the flash crash, these traders contributed to it by demanding "immediacy" ahead of other market participants (Kirilenko et al., 2014). Immediacy absorption activity of HFTs results in price adjustments that are costly to all non-HF traders, including the traditional market makers. In 2014, a flash crash in the US Treasuries market also drew attention to the influence of HFT strategies in fixed income markets. An assessment of the event indicated that the combination of high HFT activity and low market depth likely amplified the price dynamics (Bouveret et al., 2015). There is evidence that, during the 2016 flash crash of the British pound, hybrid firms that employ HFT technology and strategies, or provide direct electronic access (DEA) to HFTs, contributed to extreme price volatility. Evidence from researchers at the U.K. Financial Conduct Authority found that such traders initially trade against the direction of the initial price movement, but subsequently tend to follow and exacerbate the price change (Aquilina, et. al., 2018).

These incidents illustrate that the role of PTFs can temporarily increase volatility when liquidity is most needed. Recent research suggests that these episodes seem to have in common the fact that illiquidity brings more illiquidity, contrary to the dynamic that in normal market conditions supply and demand for liquidity are shaped by risking pricing, which can have a a self-stabilising effect. By contrast, in a crash, an increase in illiquidity fosters a disorderly run that accentuates the downward price movements (Cespa and Vives, 2017).

Thus, the key issue is whether these PTFs and HFT strategies at traditional broker-dealers could lead to greater disruption and volatility. While their strategies have not caused havoc on the system yet, during a period of abundant central bank liquidity and market confidence, questions arise regarding their behaviours that could to amplify stress (BIS, 2017). In this regard, perhaps the biggest concern is that market traders, both retail and institutional, have growing concerns about the reliability of market liquidity, which could make the markets more prone to risk aversion amid bouts of volatility.[19] This, in short, increases avenues of contagion during periods of crisis. However, given the growth of these market intermediaries and influence of their strategies in important markets, recently new forms of regulation are being applied in some markets, such as in Japan and the European Union.

Crypto-assets

One of the effects of the sharp loss of public trust in financial markets after the crisis was the search by some participants for alternate marketplaces (Blundell-Wignall, 2014). For various reasons, demand among a portion of market participants was driven by technologies that would not rely on centralised bodies, including authorities and global banks, to provide trust to the transactions, to approve and record transactions. Also, in some cases, a portion of market participants sought to delink the value of such transferrable assets from the direct influence of central banks.

Figure 1.10. Market capitalisation of selected crypto-assets, 2013-2018

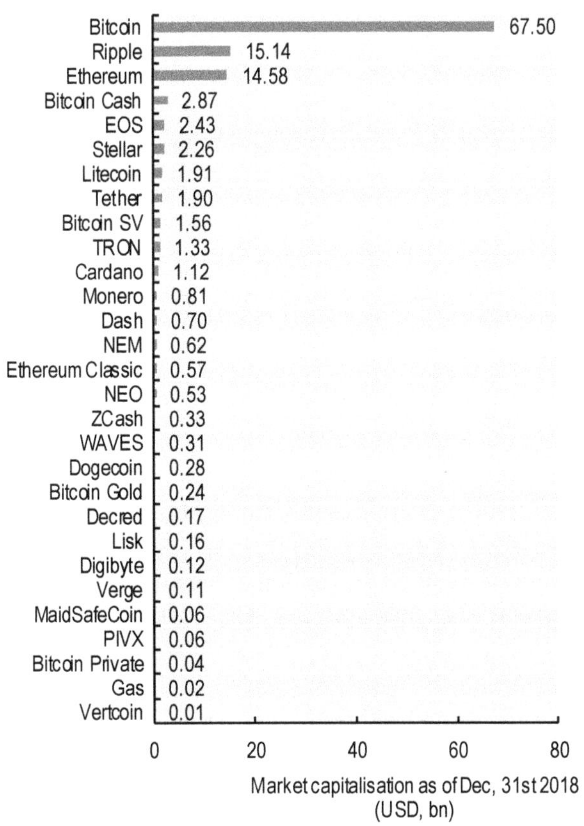

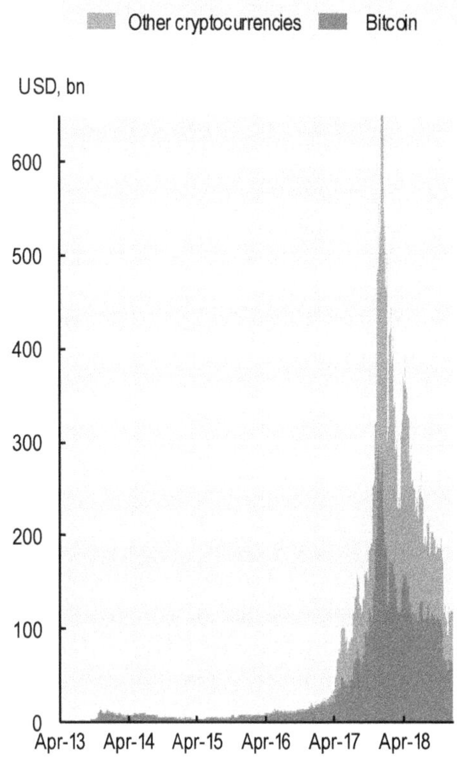

Source: Refinitiv, Coinmetrics, OECD calculations.

In the post-crisis era, these societal demands gave rise to tradable crypto-assets, backed by a distributed ledger technology referred to as blockchain. The features of blockchain allow for ledgers of the transaction and related asset information to be distributed across all parties in the network, such that the blockchain then becomes a permanent, immutable record the transactions. In this regard, the benefits of blockchain include transparency, traceability, and a greater level of trust (OECD, 2018c). In this manner, this technology helped foster the development of crypto-assets for payment and unit of account, bringing benefits to participants in the crypto-markets.

In light of these developments, trading of crypto-assets resulted in sharp increases in crypto-asset valuations, such that the entire market rose from under USD 10 billion in 2015 to peak at nearly USD 700 billion in 2017 (Figure 1.10), as Bitcoin alone rose to a market capitalisation of USD 300 billion. In the wake of several market incidents, and following various communications by market authorities raising concerns over the trading and resilience of the pricing in the crypto-asset markets, valuations have fallen considerably.

In response to the shortcomings in these forms of crypto-assets, in 2019 there has been an increase in industry announcements to issue so-called "stablecoins", which are crypto-assets that are pegged or backed by real assets such as commodities or fiat currencies. The intention of anchoring to real assets is to reduce volatility and to increase public trust in the currency-like qualities of such digital assets. The developers of the crypto-assets labelled "stablecoins" seek to reduce volatility by anchoring the "coin" to a reference asset (e.g. a sovereign currency) or a basket of assets. While the actual use of stablecoins has been limited, several new stablecoin initiatives launched by global financial institutions and large technology companies ("BigTech") suggests the potential for widespread international adoption, with its benefits and risks.

Therefore, the instability of the uncollatoralised crypto-asset markets and the uncertainty over new stablecoin plans, raise the need for more vigilant monitoring and coordination of policy responses.[20]

Various analyses of crypto-asset markets highlight challenges including rapid market developments and the fragmented nature of the markets; lack of transparency (including the identity and location of token issuers); and data gaps that hamper proper assessment of risks (FSB, 2018). Moreover, the debate over crypto-assets has drawn attention of policy makers to give further consideration to centralised digital currencies backed by central banks.

1.4.2. Financial technology outlook

As the adoption of fintech technologies continues, there is considerable potential for these innovations to bring lasting impact to quality and diversity of services, cost and overall productivity. Given concerns over flagging productivity in advanced and emerging market economies in the post-crisis era, a technology-driven productivity boost would have reinforcing benefits (BCG, 2018); McKinsey, 2018a); contributing to economic and wage growth that can support higher societal trust.

However, since the development and adoption of innovative technologies also bring potential risks, continued structural changes in the financial sector, combined with periods of heightened market volatility and market stress, could expose underlying vulnerabilities associated with financial innovations.

Despite contributing to extreme volatility during flash crashes, thus far algo-HFT strategies have not been the primary cause of the crashes, and affected markets have eventually stabilised. Market-stabilising behaviours have occurred during an era of highly accommodative monetary policy and benign credit conditions, in which a sharp fall in asset prices disconnected by fundamentals would invite value or arbitrage investors to profit from low valuations. Also, the effective use of policy tools, such as trading circuit breakers on exchanges, have helped restore market order, although at times they have been indicated for exacerbating financial market volatility.

However, during periods of heightened uncertainty amid more fragile market liquidity conditions, it is conceivable that trigger events, such as a large default or a significant operational failure, could create negative feedback dynamics that result in extreme price movements, which could contribute to contagion across markets. In this regard, the rapid shift of some PTFs from liquidity providers to liquidity consumers, particularly around unexpected events, could destabilise markets and contribute to a sharp drying up of liquidity (Hautschm et al., 2018). Though a downside risk, a major occurrence of this type could contribute to concerns over market resilience of trading platforms and exchanges.[21] Market participants that rely on stable market liquidity for their market-intermediation business are raising concerns that, amid a normalisation of monetary policy that reduces liquidity in the system and causes shifts in liquidity demand, the impact of algo/HFT could lead to more severe bouts of contagion (Kolanovic, 2018). With increasing frequency, authorities have been raising concerns over the potential impact of algorithmic and high frequency trading in ways that could exacerbate market volatility and destabilise price discovery mechanisms, eroding trust in the financial markets.

The growth of crypto-assets as a medium of exchange and the sharp volatility of decentralised crypto-assets suggests that the further growth of the market may need to evolve in ways that could build trust among investors and users. In this manner, the development of stablecoins, which seek to address aspects of this instability by being pegged to fiat currencies or traded assets such as commodities, indicates that the structure of the crypto-assets being offered is in a transformational phase. New developments may give rise to exuberance, but also to additional uncertainty regarding their impact on liquidity in traditional markets and questions over their encroachment on implicit or explicit financial safety net (such as central bank liquidity backstops).

1.4.3. Implications for trust of FinTech

Overall, public trust in these innovations could prove to be fragile. Should some incidents of product malfunctioning, security breaches and/or fraud occur give rise to perceptions that taint otherwise transformative technologies.

Given the heightened regulatory scrutiny to algo/HFT in light of periodic market disruptions, algo/HFT contribution to a more pronounced and debilitating flash crash could raise investor and public concern over the efficacy of existing policies to sufficiently address the extent of vulnerabilities in electronic trading and the rise of PTFs.

Also, while substantial losses in crypto-asset markets did not appear to spill over to securities markets, further developments and interlinkages through futures markets and cross-asset collateralisation could lead to greater disruptions in the future. The investing public may find that, at least in some jurisdictions, regulatory engagement that relies on monitoring and light-touch treatment may need enhancements. This may be of particular concern where new forms of stablecoins could be considered viable alternatives to fiat currency for international payments, trading, and a store of value.

The potential for these risks, should they emerge, to hinder progress may warrant further consideration from policy makers.[22] The challenge is to find ways to both secure and further distribute the benefits, while avoiding the hazards to the markets and financial consumers (OECD, 2018b).

1.5. Consequences and policy considerations

1.5.1. Consequences and implications for trust

Growing fragilities in debt, market-based finance and financial innovations in fixed-income and digital markets, are often manageable in periods of economic growth, but have much more serious consequences amid sharply deteriorating economic and credit conditions, and when uncertainties over policy actions arise. The OECD Economic Outlook 2019 notes that the economic outlook remains weak and there are many downside risks that cast a dark shadow over the global economy and people's well-being (OECD, 2019a). Moreover, the global economy remains largely dependent on persistent policy support. Ten years after the financial crisis, with subdued inflation, central bank balance sheets remain at unprecedented levels, interest rates are historically low, and government debt, except for a few cases, is much larger. Moreover, private sector debt is growing fast in major economies, and the quality of debt has been deteriorating, including a heightened stock of leveraged loans.

Should global economic growth and credit conditions continue to deteriorate, a new bout of financial stress could erupt, the financial markets could become more vulnerable to episodes of contagion (OECD, 2019a). Deteriorating credit conditions that contribute to higher corporate credit defaults would in turn affect funds holding speculative bonds and loans, and CLO tranche structures would be tested. Moreover, rising volatility and uncertainty could augment the impact of future flash crashes that aggravate selling pressures across multiple markets. Finally, increased risk-aversion could extract liquidity from at least some crypto-asset markets, and impose real losses to end users.

While resilient financial systems are able to withstand fluctuating investor sentiment without affecting trust, several factors raised in this chapter could erode public trust in markets, under severe conditions, including:

- Outcomes that result in unpredictably high and widespread losses across major fixed income asset classes, particularly where monetary policy incentivised a reach for higher-yielding and higher duration assets;
- Protracted debt market stress that reduces market access, raises financing costs, and in turn affects the public through offsetting mechanisms, including (government) higher taxes or lower services; (corporate) lower capital investment and job growth;
- A sharp decline in exuberance in non-bank financial intermediation where heightened liquidity transformation occurred, or where deteriorating credit quality and weaker structures incentivised excessive risk taking;
- Incidents in which market disruptions from widespread adoption of financial technologies raise concerns over market integrity;
- The extent to which these factors cause a deterioration of sustainable and inclusive economic growth.

Should a constellation of market developments cause the erosion of public trust, it could have a wide range of consequences in terms of market engagement, including market depth, cost of credit, and supply of liquidity. It could also contribute to higher aversion to market products in market-based finance, such as ETFs and liquid alternative funds, which could raise the cost of transacting. The erosion of trust could also impact the way that consumers of financial services engage with financial adaptations and innovations.

Moreover, if financial stress were to be amplified across markets and financial institutions, events could draw scrutiny to the unevenness of the implementation of post-crisis financial reforms. Furthermore, a sharp erosion of societal trust could hinder policy makers' future efforts to employ tools that impose costs or require legislative approval (OECD, 2017).

Public institutions – including central banks, fiscal authorities, regulators and enforcement authorities – have a number of ways to help safeguard against the erosion of public trust in markets, particularly during periods of market turbulence that may expose underlying structural fragilities. As well, there is room for greater attention by financial and business leaders with respect to principles and guidance, corporate culture, conduct, and balanced attention to the needs of various direct and societal stakeholders.

1.5.2. Policy considerations

The following policy considerations seek to address the potential fragilities in each of the covered market segments, to help safeguard resilience and public trust:

Fixed income markets and debt

Authorities with systemic risk oversight could give greater attention to the potential risks of high and/or rising debt levels in their financial stability assessments, and more formally link the systemic concerns to the stance of monetary policy.[23] Given the potential of quantitative easing to contribute to elevated asset valuations and high debt levels over an extended period, these experiences should be more formally specified where maintaining financial stability is part of the central banks' mandate. Recent developments of GDP-at-risk models at some central banks hold promise for incorporating economic and financial risks so that monetary policy makers better understand the consequences these trade-offs (e.g. policies that promote economic growth and lower unemployment at the expense of greater downside risks due to asset mispricing and higher debt).

Sovereign debt

The link between sovereign debt management and public trust is important for the functioning and liquidity of the debt markets, upon which pricing for other traded risk products occur. Principles of sound public debt management are followed to strengthen the international financial architecture, promote policies and practices that contribute to market stability and transparency, and reduce countries' external vulnerabilities.

In this regard, the IMF-World Bank Revised Guidelines for Public Debt Management offer guidance that is increasingly pertinent in a rising rate environment (IMF, 2014). Principles on debt management strategy and risk frameworks should be given careful consideration to ensure the appropriate balance between minimising funding costs and addressing refinancing risks, including under periods of acute market stress.

Also, in case of an illiquidity concern, sovereign debt managers are encouraged to take additional proactive steps to address potential risks associated with deteriorating market liquidity (OECD, 2019b).

Corporate debt

In the case of corporate debt, a collective action problem arises because there is no clear public oversight over the levels of corporate debt and their implications, notwithstanding systemic surveillance of financial stability risks. Market-based forces for restraining excessive corporate debt, which have functioned well in the era of modern finance, have shown signs of excessive exuberance, which suggests that market forces may not function effectively to serve as a restraining force during periods of highly accommodative monetary policy.

Thus, in order to address rising debt levels more proactively to prevent systemic risks, it is important to communicate the level of risk concerns by central authorities, so that markets can better interpret the implications for the corporate credit markets. For example, when systemic risk authorities raise concerns about the growth of debt and leveraged loans, rating agencies, asset managers and institutional investors may benefit from guidance to incorporate these concerns into their investment strategies and risk management. Such guidance might serve as a soft tool to help strengthen central bank communications on potential systemic risks of debt.

In this respect, greater use of early warnings by systemic risk bodies – within central banks or as a multi-authority bodies – should be used to flag credit concerns early in the cycle so that market participants are more attuned to the potential risks, and can price the debt accordingly.

Since micro and macroprudential tools for banking systems can contribute to a shift to market-based lending, additional tools are needed to ensure that overall corporate debt levels can be contained when stability risks arise. Leveraged loan guidance by some authorities have had limited effect because the syndication has shifted to market-based finance to avoid the leverage restrictions. Thus, enhanced regulation would need to also give consideration to the use of loans in funds, public pensions, and also CLOs.

Market-based finance

Asset managers

Over the past five years, national regulators, international organisations and standard-setting bodies have made considerable progress by engaging with the asset management industry to assess structural risks of investment funds. In this regard, the FSB and IOSCO have developed and operationalised principles to address structural vulnerabilities of asset management activities (FSB, 2017a; IOSCO, 2018). Efforts are being taken by some authorities to incorporate these into regulations where appropriate.

To solidify this progress, full and consistent implementation of the recommendations is important. International peer reviews by international organisations and standard-setting bodies of the operationalisation of these recommendations could assess the consistency of adoption across jurisdictions.

Also, authorities may further consider the use of system-wide market liquidity simulations to better understand the resilience of fixed income markets, particularly where open-ended funds and ETFs are prevalent and where broker-dealer intermediation is less resilient due, among other factors, to regulatory reforms. That said, care should be taken to also incorporate the behaviours of the range of large asset owners, to ensure a balanced perspective across the financial ecosystem (Blackrock, 2017). Results could be published so that market participants are better informed of the level of financial authorities' concerns over potential risks, which in turn would help guide investment fund managers in formulating prudent liquidity strategies.

Regulators should further assess the potential downside risks, to also understand how ETFs in less liquidity markets (e.g. fixed income, emerging markets) might perform under severe market stress. This knowledge would better help ETF sponsors, APs and investors better understand the range of potential outcomes to guide their own behaviours and risk decisions. Liquidity risk practices of ETFs, and the disclosure of APs with respect to their obligations and activities on behalf of the ETFs, could be further assessed to determine if any additional policy consideration is needed.

CLOs

To the extent that regulators in the United States and Europe sought to strengthen the rules and not inhibit further growth of the market, the unprecedented exuberance in the CLO market suggests this balance needs further calibration. Thus, risk-retention rules with respect to securitisation of CLOs could be reviewed and strengthened. Authorities may consider ways to ensure that CLO managers' interests are sufficiently aligned other tranche holders to incentivise due diligence and prudence in managing the risks throughout the credit cycle.

Market regulators should closely scrutinise the marketing of CLO tranches into products that are sold to retail investors, such as open-ended funds, or to smaller institutional investors that may not have the sophisticated in-house analytical capabilities.

Rating agency methodologies for CLOs could give further consideration to plausible default and recovery rates of covenant light loans during severe credit stress, and also to underlying assumptions of market liquidity.

Financial innovations

Given the increasing frequency of severe market incidents in which algo/HFT behaviour exacerbates price volatility, potential severity of spillovers in less-liquid markets is cause for concern. As some major central banks have raised concerns that the amplification of market risks due to HFT could have financial stability consequences, a greater understanding of the strategies, impact and interconnectedness is warranted. Moreover, greater understanding of the diversity of business models are needed.

Such analysis at the national and global levels would arm policy makers with greater ability to consider appropriate micro and macroprudential measures, where needed. For example, regulators may wish to assess the algorithms and strategies of large independent players, and to simulate how, under some circumstances, interactions with other market intermediaries could lead to highly disruptive market spillovers.

Taken together, these recommended areas could be considered by policy makers and corporate leaders, were applicable, to help improve financial market resilience in ways that fundamentally safeguard both investors' and the public's trust.

Notes

[1] For a description of the importance of trust and investor optimism as two key components of investor confidence, see Ko (2017). Optimism relates to prospects for asset portfolio returns and variances including a temporal assessment of investment prospects based mostly on economic and business fundamentals.

[2] The efficient markets hypothesis, developed by Eugene Fama, states that asset prices fully reflect all available information. This necessitates fair disclosure regimes that are based on timely and broad dissemination of financial reports that are accurate.

[3] Market participants include investors (institutional and retail), issuers, intermediaries that engage in market making and facilitating the process of credit intermediation, and other entities that support this process. The distinction between such participants and the general public is that the latter includes portions of society that are not actively engaged in the markets, but nevertheless expect that financial markets serve the broader good, from supporting economic growth, jobs creation, and positive spillovers to other parts of society.

[4] See BIAC (2019),"Statement to OECD Ministerial Council Meeting May 2019: Top 10 business priorities." It is clear that digitalisation offers unprecedented opportunities to raise efficiency and productivity, enable creativity and innovation, and increase competition and consumer welfare, while fostering social and economic progress.

[5] With respect to corporate profitability, see Correa-Caro et al. (2018).

[6] It should be noted that a rise in interest rates linked to an increase in economic growth, all else equal, would be accompanied by an increase in government revenues. The impact of this adjustment in growth and cost of financing could, on net, be positive on public balances, despite the increase in debt burden.

[7] See Blanchard for discussion of how high sovereign debt levels could remain sustainable as long as long as very low interest rates persist. Olivier Blanchard, 2019. "Public Debt and Low Interest Rates," American Economic Review, vol 109(4), pages 1197-1229.

[8] Risk-adjusted book-value of returns can be considered to be the actual return on equity minus the cost of equity, based on the CAPM model.

[9] See additional papers from the IMF-BIS-OECD Conference on "Weak productivity: the role of financial factors and policies", January 2018, www.bis.org/events/bis_imf_oecd_jan18_conf.htm. Also, several academic papers suggest highly accommodative monetary policy shifts investment into corporates with lower productivity.

[10] Various measures of outstanding amounts reflect estimates based on the callable/convertible nature of the CoCos. This estimate is roughly 70% of the total CoCo bonds issued over the past five years. Bologna et al. (2018) calculates total European CoCos outstanding at USD 133 bn euros, roughly equal to the total issued over the past five years.

[11] "Under many circumstances sovereign debt markets may be considered as a safe haven during periods of heightened uncertainty and market volatility. However, where the sovereign conditions or sovereign market risk are in question, this may not be the case, and sovereign debt markets could transmit risk to other markets such as the bank funding markets. Evidence suggests that European sovereign debt markets exhibited aspects of flight to safety prior to the sovereign debt crisis, and more acute debt-related contagion during the financial crisis when some nations debt sustainability came under investor scrutiny. See Beirne, J. and M.Fratzscher, 2013. "The pricing of sovereign risk and contagion during the European sovereign debt crisis. ECB Working Paper Series N°1625, https://www.ecb.europa.eu/pub/pdf/scpwps/ecbwp1625.pdf.

[12] For further consideration of the impact of market losses on pension plans, see Yermo and Severinson (2008).

[13] Funds in certain jurisdictions, including the United States, are required to have liquidity risk management programmes that are designed, among other things, to mitigate the potential adverse effects of large redemptions on remaining shareholders, whether motivated by first mover advantage or other reasons.

[14] For example, see the Federal Reserve's use of liquidity facilities to address failures in market-based finance: https://www.federalreserve.gov/monetarypolicy/bst_crisisresponse.htm.

[15] The reader should note that this section focuses on CLOs rather than the underlying leveraged loan market, which is much larger at roughly 2.3 trillion, according to Thomson Reuters estimates. The reason for less emphasis on the leveraged loan market is that it, unlike the investment grade

tranches of CLOs is inherently risky as a market of entirely non-investment grade credits. Therefore, losses due to direct exposure to leveraged loans or leveraged loan funds are to be expected, and there is presumably less of an issue of trust. By contrast, the structuring of products that transform these risky assets into AAA tranches, and are rated as such, are the source of a potential trust deficit.

[16] Various sources, including rating agencies, market sources, and regulatory analysis. See the Federal Reserve (2019); Bank of England (2018); Pinebridge (2017); NAIC (2018).

[17] In 2014, the Loan Syndications and Trading Association sued the SEC and the Federal Reserve to exempt open-market CLOs from the rules, since, among other factors, CLO managers do not originate the loans they securitise. In early 2018, a US Court of Appeals unanimously ruled that risk-retention rules for securitisations should not apply to CLOs. CLO managers are not required to retain a portion of the CLOs they manage. See US Court of Appeal decision: https://www.cadc.uscourts.gov/internet/opinions.nsf/871D769D4527442A8525822F0052E1E9/$file/17-5004-1717230.pdf.

[18] The Autorité des Marchés Financiers (AMF) published a detailed analysis of the activity of market participants engaged in high-frequency trading (HFT) on CAC 40 stocks, with focus on their presence in the order book, how they provide and consume liquidity and how their behaviour changes during periods of intense stress. See AMF (2017).

[19] Central banks' research notes that PTF liquidity absorbing behaviours amid market turbulence, causes the risk of excessive volatility to increase, thereby provoking market turmoil. See Bundesbank (2016).

[20] There are several international coordination efforts with respect to FinTech and stablecoins. The OECD is exploring benefits, risks and policy responses through its Committee on Financial Markets, and through its annual Blockchain Policy Forum. Also, the G7 is assessing the potential risks from global stablecoin adoption.

[21] Office of Financial Research (2018), see explanation on market volatility and principal trading firms. See also, Salmon (2017).

[22] Philippon et al. (2017). FinTech can improve both financial stability and access to services, but this requires certain changes in the focus of regulations.

[23] OECD (2010). See recommendation I.C with respect to surveillance and analysis, and II.C with respect to establishment of an accountability framework.

References

Aquilina, M., B. Eyles, J. Shao and C. Ysusi (2018), "How do participants behave during Flash events? Evidence from the UK equity market", Financial Conduct Authority.

AMF (2017), "Study of the behaviour of high-frequency traders on Euronext Paris", Risks and Trends, Autorité des Marchés Financiers.

Auerbach, A. J. and Y. Gorodnichenk (2017), "Fiscal Stimulus and Fiscal Sustainability", *NBER Working Paper* No. 23789.

Bank of England (2018), "Who invests in securitisations of leveraged loans?", Financial Stability Report, No. 44, November.

Baranova, Y., J. Coen, P. Lowe, J. Noss and L. Silvestri (2017), "Simulating stress across the financial system: the resilience of corporate bond markets and the role of investment funds", Bank of England, Financial Stability Paper No. 42.

Beqiraj, E., S. Fedeli and F. Forte (2018), "Public debt sustainability: An empirical study on OECD countries", *Journal of Macroeconomics*, Volume 58.

BIS (2017), "The sterling 'flash event' of 7 October 2016", Report prepared by an ad-hoc Markets Committee working group.

BIS (2016), "Hanging Up the Phone: electronic trading of fixed income", *BIS Quarterly Review*, March.

Blackrock (2017), "A Macroprudential Response to Risks in the Asset Management Sector", Speech by Barbara Novick, Vice Chairman. Frankfurt, Germany, May.

Blanchard, O. (2019), "Public Debt and Low Interest Rates", *American Economic Review*, vol 109(4), pages 1197-1229, http://doi.org/10.1257/aer.109.4.1197.

Blundell-Wignall, A. (2014), "Bitcoin Question: Currency vs Trustless Transfer Technology", *OECD Working Papers on Finance, Insurance and Private Pensions* No.37, OECD Publishing.

Boermans M. and S. Wijnbergen (2017), "Contingent convertible bonds: Who invests in European CoCos?", *Applied Economics Letters*, 25(4), pp. 234-238.

Bologna, P., A. Miglietta and A. Segura (2018), "Contagion in the European Coco Market", CEPR Policy Portal, https://voxeu.org/article/contagion-european-cocos-market.

Boston Consulting Group (2018), "FinTech in Capital Markets 2018: Boosting Productivity through Capital Innovation", White Paper, March.

Bouveret, A., P. Breuer, Y. Chen, D. Jones and T. Sasaki (2015), "Fragilities in the U.S. Treasury Market: Lessons from the 'Flash Rally' of 15 October 2014", IMF Working Paper.

Bundesbank (2016), "High-frequency trading can amplify financial market volatility", Monatsbericht.

Çelik, S., G. Demirtaş and M. Isaksson (2019), "Corporate Bond Markets in a Time of Unconventional Monetary Policy", OECD Capital Market Series, Paris, www.oecd.org/corporate/Corporate-Bond-Markets-in-a-Time-of-Unconventional-Monetary-Policy.htm.

Central Bank of Ireland (2017), "Exchange-traded Funds", Discussion Paper, May.

Cespa, G. and X. Vives (2017), "High frequency trading and fragility", *ECB Working Paper Series*.

Cetorelli, N., F. Duarte and T. Eisenbach (2016), "Are Asset Managers Vulnerable to Fire Sales?", Federal Reserve Bank of New York, Liberty Street Economics Blog, https://libertystreeteconomics.newyorkfed.org/2016/02/are-asset-managers-vulnerable-to-fire-sales.html.

Correa-Caro, C., L. Medina, M. Poplawski-Riberio and B. Sutton (2018), "Fiscal Stimulus Impact on Firms' Profitability during the Global Financial Crisis", *IMF Working Paper Series*.

Edelman (2018), 2018 Edelman Trust Barometer, www.edelman.com/research/2018-edelman-trust-barometer.

Federal Reserve (2019), "Financial Stability Report", May.

Federal Reserve (2014), "Six agencies jointly approve final risk retention rule", Press Release, October.

Freedman, C., M. Kumhof, D. Laxton, D. Muir and S. Mursula (2010), "Global Effects of Fiscal Stimulus During the Crisis", *Journal of Monetary Economics*, 57(5), pp. 506-526.

FSB (2018), "Crypto-asset markets: Potential channels for future financial stability implications", October.

FSB (2017a), "Policy recommendations to address structural vulnerabilities from asset management activities", Policy Documents, January.

FSB (2017b), "Shadow banking recommendations to the German G20 Presidency", March 2018.

Guggenheim Investments (2018), "High-Yield and Bank Loan Outlook: Late-Cycle Boost and Boom", Perspectives Sector Views, September, www.guggenheiminvestments.com/perspectives/sector-views/q3-2018-high-yield-and-bank-loan-outlook.

Hautschm N., M. Noé and S. Zhang (2018), "The Ambivalent Role of High-Frequency Trading in Turbulent Market Periods", *CFS Working Paper Series* 580, Center for Financial Studies (CFS).

IMF (2014), "Revised Guidelines for Public Debt Management", IMF Policy Paper, April.

IOSCO (2018), "Recommendations and good practices to improve liquidity risk management for investment funds", February.

Kim, S., M. Plosser and J. Santos (2016), "Did the Supervisory Guidance on Leveraged Lending Work?", Federal Reserve Bank of New York, Liberty Street Economics Blog, https://libertystreeteconomics.newyorkfed.org/2016/05/did-the-supervisory-guidance-on-leveraged-lending-work.html.

Kirilenko, A., M. Kyle and S. T. Tuzun (2014), "The Flash Crash: The Impact of High Frequency Trading on an Electronic Market", *SSRN Electronic Journal*, 10.2139/ssrn.1686004.

Ko, K. J. (2017), "Economics Note – Investor Confidence", SEC DERA briefing note.

Kolanovic, M. (2018), "Ten years after the financial crisis", JPMorgan Research.

McKinsey (2018a), "FinTech decoded: The Capital Markets Infrastructure Opportunity", Insights, www.mckinsey.com/industries/financial-services/our-insights/fintech-decoded-the-capital-markets-infrastructure-opportunity.

McKinsey (2018b), "Rising Corporate Debt, Perils or Promise?", McKinsey Global Institute, Discussion Paper, June.

Morris, I. S. and H. Shin (2017), "Redemption Risk and Cash Hoarding by Asset Managers", BIS, Working Paper No. 608.

NAIC (2018), "US insurance industry exposure to CLOs", Capital Markets Special Report, August.

Nickel, C. and A. Tudyka (2013), "Fiscal stimulus in times of high debt: reconsidering multipliers and twin deficits", *ECB Working Paper Series*.

OECD (2019a), *OECD Economic Outlook*, Volume 2019 Issue 1: Preliminary version, OECD Publishing, Paris, https://doi.org/10.1787/b2e897b0-en.

OECD (2019b), *OECD Sovereign Borrowing Outlook 2019*, OECD Publishing, Paris, https://doi.org/10.1787/aa7aad38-en.

OECD (2018a), *OECD Compendium of Productivity Indicators 2018*, OECD Publishing, Paris, https://doi.org/10.1787/pdtvy-2018-en.

OECD (2018b), "Framework for Digitalisation in Finance", Financial Markets, Insurance and Pensions: Digitalisation and Finance, www.oecd.org/finance/financial-markets-insurance-and-pensions-2018.htm.

OECD (2018c), "OECD and the blockchain revolution", Speech by Greg Medcraft, March.

OECD (2017), "Trust and Public Policy: How Better Governance Can Help Rebuild Public Trust", *OECD Public Governance Reviews*, OECD Publishing, Paris, https://doi.org/10.1787/9789264268920-en.

OECD (2015), *OECD Business and Finance Outlook 2015*, OECD Publishing, Paris, https://doi.org/10.1787/9789264234291-en.

OECD (2010), "Policy framework for effective and efficient financial regulation: General guidance and high-level checklist", *OECD Journal: Financial Market Trends*, vol. 2009/2, https://doi.org/10.1787/fmt-2009-5kmn0vkxwng1.

OECD (2009) "Report on the Strategic Response: Strategies for Aligning Stimulus Measures with Long-term Growth", Reports submitted to the OECD's annual ministerial meeting in June 2009.

Office of Financial Research (2018. "Annual Report to Congress", November.

Patalano, R. and C. Roulet (2019), "Structural Developments in Global Financial Intermediation", *OECD Working Papers on Finance, Insurance and Private Pensions*, OECD Publishing, Paris (forthcoming).

Philippon T. and A. Salo (2017), "Bail-ins and Bank Resolution in Europe: A Progress Report", International Center for Monetary and Banking Studies, *Geneva Reports on the World Economy* Special Report 4, CEPR.

PIMCO (2018), "Investing in a Negative Interest Rate World", Investment Education, https://global.pimco.com/en-gbl/resources/education/investing-in-a-negative-interest-rate-world.

Pinebridge Investments (2017), "Seeing Beyond the Complexity: An Introduction to Collateralized Loan Obligations".

Reinhart, C., M. and K. S. Rogoff (2008), "This Time is Different: A Panoramic View of Eight Centuries of Financial Crises", NBER Working Paper No. 13882.

Salmon, C. (2017), "Keeping up with Fast Markets", Bank of England, Speech at 13th Annual Central Bank Conference on the Microstructure of Financial Markets, London, October.

S&P Ratings (2018), "Leveraged Loans: Another New Record for Covenant-Lite", News and Insights, www.spglobal.com/marketintelligence/en/news-insights/latest-news-headlines/leveraged-loan-news/leveraged-loans-another-new-record-for-covenant-lite.

Taylor, J. B. (2018), "Fiscal Stimulus Programs during the Great Recession", Hoover Workshop Series on the 2008 Financial Crisis, December.

Yermo, J. and C. Severinson (2008), "The Impact of the Financial Crisis on Defined Benefit Plans and the Need for Countercyclical Funding Regulations", *OECD Working Papers on Finance, Insurance and Private Pensions* N°3, OECD Publishing, Paris, https://doi.org/10.1787/5km91p3jszxw-en.

Chapter 2. Trust and financial institutions

Population ageing, low returns on retirement savings, low growth, less stable employment careers, and insufficient pension coverage among some groups of workers: These trends have eroded the belief that pension systems are managed with workers' best interests in mind and that they will deliver on their promises, once workers reach retirement age. This chapter considers three policy objectives to win back trust in financial institutions: promoting prudent pension management and supporting pension funds' fiduciary duties; enhancing financial consumer protection; and addressing environmental and social risks.

2.1. Introduction

In the wake of the financial crisis of 2008, trust in financial institutions amongst consumers and society more broadly plummeted. In the United States, for example, trust in the financial sector dropped to 36% in 2009, from 69% in 2008 (Edelman, 2009). Globally, the financial services sector achieved an 11 percentage point increase in trust in the five years from 2012, but it is still one of the least trusted industries with just 54% of consumers reporting that they trusted the sector in 2017 (Edelman, 2017).

For consumers and society to have trust in institutions, those institutions must be competent and effective in delivering on their goals. They must also operate consistently with a set of values that reflect citizens' expectations of integrity and fairness.

This chapter focuses on ways in which policies can promote increased trust in financial institutions by ensuring the safety of assets, fair treatment of customers and meeting the expectations of society. Three specific elements are considered: policies that promote prudent pension management; policies designed to enhance financial consumer protection; and policies to address environmental and social risks.[1] It explains how such policies can help financial institutions in responding to the preferences of their beneficiaries and consumers, promote long term value creation and avoid potential negative commercial impacts associated with environmental and social risks.

Trust on pension systems delivering pensions, and trust on pension funds managing people's retirement savings in their best interest, is low. Population ageing, the financial and economic crisis, and the current environment of low growth and low returns is making people doubt whether pension systems and pension funds will deliver on their promises, whether they are run with their best interest in mind, and whether they will get adequate pensions.

There is also a low level of trust in pension fund management, which stems from a lack of appropriate governance, clearly stated missions, and adequate investment policies and risk management. International significant pension fund and policy makers are developing best practices which can help overcome some of these issues.

Policies to enhance financial consumer protection are important to promote and support trust and confidence in the financial system. While much attention has been paid to regulations relating to the conduct of financial institutions, by themselves they do not necessarily result in increased trust. In more recent times, attention has also been focused on issues relating to conflicts of interest, culture and the governance of financial products themselves.

Additionally, demand from clients and beneficiaries for financial institutions to consider environmental and social factors in their decision-making is growing. The role of financial institutions in avoiding negative impacts on society and the environment is also increasingly recognised as an important factor towards driving commercial performance, economic stability and global sustainability objectives.

The themes focused on in this chapter are selected from a constellation of possible approaches policy makers can consider to build trust in financial institutions. Governments' roles in supporting trust in both the financial sector and the economy, more broadly, are discussed in other chapters, including through promoting trust in financial markets (Chapter 1), trust in law enforcement (Chapter 3) and trust in online markets (Chapter 5).

2.2. Policy options to improve trust in pension institutions

People's trust in pension systems is lacking with many questioning whether they will get a pension when they retire and whether that pension will be adequate to maintain their standard of living. This loss of confidence applies to all types of pension arrangements, i.e. defined benefit (DB), pay-as-you-go (PAYG) or funded pensions. They also wonder whether defined contribution (DC) funded pensions will provide adequate pensions. In addition, people are concerned about whether the institutions managing their retirement savings (e.g. pension funds) are doing so in their best interest. They also question whether the fees that pension funds charge for managing their retirement saving are aligned with the actual cost of managing their retirement savings and they are not being overcharged. Finally, the growth of pension arrangements in which people need to make many decisions and bear most of the risks (e.g. investment and longevity risk), DC plans, means that people need guidance to make those decisions and address those risks. In this context, the design of DC plans need to improve accounting for behavioural biases and low financial knowledge that make people decision making a struggle. In addition, financial advisors may be exposed to conflict of interest. The section on consumer protection deals with the issues arising from conflict of interest of retirement financial advisors and discusses potential solutions.

The lack of trust stems from the challenges that pension systems and pension funds managing people's retirement savings face. Pension systems are are being forced to adjust to meet these challenges and people often fail to understand why changes are being proposed or implemented. An effort from the authorities and other stakeholders in improving communication and comprehension of those reforms is clearly necessary.

The fallout from the financial and economic crisis, population ageing and the current economic environment characterised by low growth, low wage growth, low returns and low long-term interest rates, pensions are changing the pension landscape. These circumstances mean that current contributions and current contribution periods can no longer adequately provide the type of pensions and security that people have come to expect.

The global financial crisis has led to a reduction in the capacity of governments to finance retirement promises. People's trust in public pensions is diminishing. People are also losing confidence in private pensions with the fall in the balances accumulated in their pension funds provoked by the crisis.

Pensions are also coming under pressure as the baby boom generations retire, improvements in mortality and life expectancy, and longevity risks linked to uncertainty around future improvements in life expectancy. Living a longer and healthier life is generally good but, if not properly taken into account, population ageing challenges the financial sustainability, solvency and adequacy of pension systems. Population ageing is leading both to an increase in the number of people in retirement relative to the size of the working age population and also, most importantly, to an increase in the number of years that people spend in retirement. This increase needs to be financed.

As a result of population ageing and, in particular, the continued improvements in mortality and life expectancy, PAYG pensions face financial sustainability problems, defined benefit funded pensions need to secure their continued solvency, and defined contribution (DC) pensions need to consider ways to ensure that individuals have an adequate income during retirement. Contributing more and for longer periods, especially by postponing retirement as life expectancy increases, is the best approach to face these challenges.

Pension funds and annuity providers are exposed to longevity risk owing to uncertainty about future improvements in mortality and life expectancy. To address the risk of unanticipated increases in liabilities, regulators and policy makers should ensure that pension funds and annuity providers use regularly updated mortality tables, which incorporate future improvements in mortality and life expectancy. The regulatory framework could also help ensure that capital markets offer additional capacity to mitigate longevity risk, by addressing the need for transparency, standardisation and liquidity. Index-based financial instruments and the publication of a longevity index to serve as a benchmark for the pricing and risk assessment of longevity hedges would be helpful in this regard. Furthermore, the regulatory framework should recognise the reduction in risk exposure these instruments offer.

The current economic environment of low returns, low interest rates, and low economic growth further compounds the problems of financial sustainability, solvency and adequacy. These factors may lead to lower resources than expected to finance retirement promises or simply lead to lower retirement income. Low returns reduce the expected future value of contributions as assets accumulated will grow at a lower rate than expected. Low interest rates may reduce the amount of pension income that a given amount of accumulated assets may be able to deliver, especially in defined contribution (DC) pensions. Additionally, low economic growth may reduce the overall resources available to finance pension promises.

In summary, population ageing, the fallout from the financial and economic crisis as well as the current environment of low growth and low interest rates may increase financial pressure on defined benefit (DB) pension arrangements, which include potential fiscal difficulties for pay-as-you-go (PAYG) financed public pension arrangements and solvency problems for funded DB pension arrangements. It may also create serious problems of retirement income adequacy for defined contribution (DC) pension arrangements in which individuals bear many of the risks of saving for retirement.

Policy makers, regulators and the pension industry have been responding to those challenges and thus addressing to some extent the potential sources of the mistrust on pensions. Policy reforms implemented in the last decade have make pension systems more robust and better placed to deliver pensions (OECD, 2018b). In particular, reforms implemented in PAYG DB public pension arrangements have made them more fiscally sustainable. Improvements in the design of DC pension plans taking into account behavioural biases and low financial knowledge is improving retirement outcomes. Additionally, recent reforms have laid the foundations for people to regain trust that pension funds will manage their retirement savings in their best interest. These reforms include more robust regulatory and supervisory frameworks, stronger governance, investment policies and strategies, investment risk management, and a more solid focus on the best interest of members, including the consideration in their investment policies of sustainable investment opportunities.

Countries have accelerated the pace of pension reforms stabilising public pension expenditure while addressing concerns about whether pensions will be adequate in ageing societies. A majority of countries have implemented reforms that have partially addressed the problems of fiscal sustainability. They have introduced automatic mechanisms to adjust pension benefits to economic and demographic realities, such as planned increases in the statutory age of retirement, and linking benefits, retirement age and/or maximum contribution periods to future improvements in life expectancy. This coupled with the strengthening of safety nets to improve poverty relief in old age, and some progress on adequacy, especially for low income socio-economic groups, have gone a long way in making public pensions sounder, but substantial gaps remain.

Pension arrangements in which assets back pension benefits, and in particular those with a direct and straightforward link between contributions and benefits, DC plans, have grown in importance. These pension plans require individuals to make many more decisions regarding their retirement. Moreover, individuals bear more risks, such as investment and longevity. This has highlighted the importance of improving the design of DC pensions taking into account behavioural biases and low financial knowledge (OECD, 2018b, Ch.5).

Box 2.1. The role of financial literacy in improving trust in pensions

Higher levels of financial literacy can contribute to trust by ensuring that people have a general understanding of the purpose of saving for retirement, the approaches that can be taken and the practicalities of putting a plan into action from the first contributions to the final stages of decumulation. Such education empowers individuals to take informed decisions, whilst also helping them to recognise the benefits of seeking professional advice when necessary and learning how, and when to trust the products and services on offer.

At the most basic level, people will not trust pension institutions if they do not readily understand that they are safeguarding their income during a potentially long period of retirement. Evidence from the United Kingdom and the United States, highlights that many people have a tendency to underestimate their expected lifespan with respect to population life tables, and that women are generally more likely than men to underestimate their likely longevity (O'Connell, 2010). If, on top of this, people do not know how to calculate their likely income needs in retirement or understand the benefit of saving from a young age, it is very likely that the industry will be poorly perceived, even when they attempt to encourage beneficial behaviours.

Depending on the structure of each pension system, financial literacy is most important in helping people to manage: i) private pensions than for public pensions; ii) personal pension plans than for occupational plans; and iii) defined-contribution (or notional defined-contribution) schemes than for defined-benefit schemes, since the latter require only limited engagement from the individual (OECD, 2016c).

Evidence suggests that knowledge of concepts necessary to perform saving calculations, such as compound interest rates, the time value of money, the difference between real and nominal values, and the principle of risk diversification, should not be taken for granted in the population at large (Atkinson and Messy, 2012]); Lusardi and Mitchell, 2011). Furthermore, surveys in various countries have shown that many savers do not know which type of private pension they have and possess limited knowledge of important characteristics of their own pension arrangements (Banks and Oldfield, 2007; Barrett, Mosca and Whelan, 2013; ILC-UK, 2015; Money and Pensions Panel, 2013). Several studies – mainly from the United States – suggest that workers are poorly informed about their private pension plans (Mitchell, 1988; Gustman and Steinmeier, 1989; Gustman and Steinmeier, 2004; Gustman, Steinmeier and Tabatabai, 2008; Dushi and Iams, 2010). Information, guidance and improved awareness campaigns would improve levels of engagement and trust in such populations.

Automatic features, default options, simple information and choice, higher level of financial literacy, and financial incentives lead to better retirement outcomes. As a result of low levels of financial knowledge and behavioural biases, people make inappropriate decisions regarding their retirement. For example, mechanisms such as automatic enrolment and escalation of contributions can harness inertia to help people participate and save more for retirement. Default options assist people unable, or unwilling, to choose a contribution rate, a pension provider, an investment strategy or a post-retirement product, to end in place that may be in their best interest. Other tools to help with decision making, include web applications, limiting options and making comparisons easier, pension statements conveying key information simply, and financial literacy seminars and financial advice to help people understand the information. Box 2.1 discusses the role of financial literacy in improving trust in pensions. Finally, financial incentives do provide an incentive to people to participate and save more. Evidence suggest that they do, and the fiscal cost may not be large, however, it needs planning to account for the fiscal room available in each country, and to focus those incentives in the different subpopulations according to their saving needs and policy objectives (OECD, 2018a).

The OECD and pension regulators have strengthened the regulatory framework of funded private pensions in response to the diminished trust of the public in private pensions. The OECD Core Principles of Private Pension Regulation (OECD, 2016d) cover all types of funded pension arrangements and strengthen the regulatory framework to make sure that funded pension arrangements work in the best interest of members, both for current retirees and for those currently saving for retirement. These principles argue that pension funds must always act in the best interest of members. This fiduciary duty should always be guaranteed in the law and in the regulatory framework.

Strengthening governance requires having regulatory and legal frameworks for pension funds at arm's length from government. Pension funds should have clearly stated missions to guide investment policy. They should have an oversight board that is accountable to the competent authorities as well as to members. The boards of pension funds should be transparent about their governance arrangements and their investment and risk management to keep them accountable to different stakeholders.

Pension funds and their boards should express their performance objectives in terms of their mission and should monitor performance against their long-term goal of providing retirement income with security and manage the funds in the best interest of members, rather than against a market benchmark. Target date and lifecycle funds tend to be the preferred investment strategies for pension funds with individual accounts (OECD, 2012a). Long-term return strategies may offer better returns, but at a higher risk that insufficient funds will be available to members at retirement. Large pension funds take into account ESG investment opportunities, but always in the context of their fiduciary duty to members.

Finally, to rebuild trust pension funds should consider aligning their fees and charges levied on employers and members with the actual cost of providing funded pension arrangements. Providing pension services involves costs such as administration and investment activities. These costs can greatly affect the ultimate value of accumulated retirement savings. Some pension arrangements can be also more expensive, such as those providing more choice. The potential impact of these charges on the ultimate value of retirement savings can be large. For example, charges of 1.5% of assets, reduces the final pot at retirement by nearly 30% as compared with a situation without charges. Charges of just 0.5% reduce retirement income by more than 11%.

Therefore, it is important that policy makers and regulators make sure that the charges paid for those services reflect the actual cost to providers. Unfortunately, market mechanisms have often been insufficient to align charges with the actual cost to providers due to market failures, such as asymmetric information or behavioural biases.

Measures to improve transparency are essential, but are not enough to align costs and charges. They work best when supported by pricing regulations (e.g. caps on fees, default investment strategies) and structural solutions (e.g. tender mechanisms and default options). To maximise net returns, policy makers and regulators can also use measures such as benchmarking and tying investment expenses more closely to portfolio performance.

Pension funds, to gain people's trust, should also consider sustainable and environmental, social and governance (ESG) investment opportunities are part of pension of their duties and investment policies. Pension funds should assess sustainable and ESG investment opportunities as any other investment opportunity by examining their risk and maintaining their mandate to manage people's retirement savings in their best interest. They should, in this context, aim at incorporating in their investment policy investment opportunities that provide in the long-term the best risk-adjusted net of costs real returns. Saving for retirement is long-term in nature, but timing of disbursement also bring in short-term liquidity considerations. Pension funds should consider all investment opportunities, including ESG opportunities, as part of their investment objective, their investment policy and risk management approaches.

The regulatory framework does not prohibit nor encourages pension funds from integrating in their investment policy and risk management ESG investment opportunities (OECD, 2017). Investors' interpretation and lack of clarity on the rules by the regulator may discourage ESG integration. The main barriers for ESG integration are practical. Lack of standardised and harmonise disclosure and of data, as well lack of models, indicators and metrics to appropriately assess ESG investment opportunities are the real problem facing pension funds to integrate ESG factors and risks in their investment policy. The section 4 of this chapter will deal further with this issue.

2.3. Financial consumer protection

Empowering and protecting consumers is also a key aspect of trust building. Financial consumer protection policies seek to promote disclosure of all information including cost and a competitive marketplace with good quality and value-for-money products. They also aim to ensure that customers receive fair treatment, are not misled or subject to misconduct, and can access to redress and compensation mechanisms when things go wrong.

The G20/OECD High Level Principles on Financial Consumer Protection (OECD, 2011a) is a well-established policy instrument setting out ten principles for a comprehensive policy framework for financial consumer protection, including in relation to responsible business conduct. While the notion of responsible business conduct covers a broad range of actions and behaviours by a financial institution, its employees and representative, at the core of the Principle is the requirement that financial services providers and authorised agents should have as an objective to work in the best interest of their customers. The Principle also relates to matters such as remuneration and incentives, avoiding conflicts and suitability.

Jurisdictions have implemented a wide range of laws and regulations governing the conduct of financial institutions, overseen by authorities with responsibility for regulating and supervising market conduct in the interests of protecting financial consumers.

Conduct risk is generally the risk of conduct occurring which does not meet applicable standards or requirements. Those standards or requirements may be those set out in laws or regulations, professional standards or unwritten standards of conduct expected by the community in which the financial institution operates. Such conduct can include inappropriate, unethical or unlawful behaviour on the part of an organisation's management or employees and is damaging to consumers' trust in the organisation. That conduct can be caused by deliberate actions or may be inadvertent, because of inadequacies in an organisation's practices or systems.

The amount of financial services regulation governing conduct has increased significantly since the global financial crisis. However, it is not clear that alone this is sufficient to rebuild public trust. For example, according to a study by PwC into the relationship between the UK financial services sector and its customers, while 49% of people believe regulation had been strengthened since the financial crisis, 57% did not believe that the reforms were sufficient to prevent history from repeating itself (PwC, 2014).

Not surprisingly, more recently, there has been an increased focus by policy makers, regulators and supervisors responsible for conduct on the culture within financial institutions and the quality of financial products being sold to financial consumers, complementary to the focus on market conduct. While appropriate rules and regulations governing conduct are important, in order for them to be properly effective and adhered to in the appropriate sprit, it is vital that the institutions subject to them are operating under a healthy culture where conflicts of interest are managed and the needs of their customers are prioritised, supported by the financial products on offer.

The OECD, via the G20/OECD Task Force on Financial Consumer Protection, is monitoring developments, from a financial consumer protection perspective, relating to culture within financial institutions and financial product governance. In this regard, it is supporting a project being conducted by the International Network on Financial Consumer Protection (FinCoNet) in collaboration the G20/OECD Task Force on Financial Consumer Protection, to understand policy and supervisory approaches to financial product governance and culture in jurisdictions around the globe. The results of this work will inform the development of international good practices. In the meantime, the following sections outline how managing conflicts of interest, culture and product governance support responsible conduct and therefore the protection of financial consumers.

2.3.1. Trust and financial advice – managing conflicts of interest

Financial advisors often serve as intermediaries between financial institutions and individuals, and thereby can directly influence the level of trust that individuals have towards these institutions. For investment advice, human interaction is highly valued, and credentialed financial advisors are viewed as the most trusted source of financial information (Edelman, 2018). At the same time, unwanted selling and the lack of transparency in the cost of financial products and services are two leading factors that lead to lower trust in financial institutions (Edelman, 2018). Therefore, it is crucial in order to maintain consumer trust in financial institutions, to ensure that financial advice is appropriate and that the cost of this advice is transparent and clear.

A key factor behind mis-selling and poor financial advice is the conflicts of interest that financial advisors face when recommending financial products to their clients. These conflicts of interest most often relate to how the advisors are compensated for providing the advice. For example, if advisors are paid through sales commissions, they have a direct incentive to recommend to their clients the product paying the highest commission, even if it may not be the best product for the client's needs.

In order to improve the quality of financial advice that individuals receive, policy makers have sought to implement measures to mitigate the conflicts of interest that financial advisors face. Three main tools are used to do this: disclosure requirements, duty of care standards, and limits on how financial advisors are remunerated (OECD, 2016).

Disclosure alone has not been effective in ensuring the best outcomes for financial consumers. Many jurisdictions require that advisors clearly disclose the cost of their advice, the nature of their remuneration, and/or any conflicts of interest that they face. However, these disclosures have historically been difficult for consumers to understand, and individuals do not necessarily think through the implications that conflicts may have for the advice they receive. Even when consumers pay attention to such disclosures, they can backfire and potentially result in worse outcomes. In some cases, consumers seem to place too much weight on this information, leading them to disregard the advice, and in others, they may feel more pressure to follow the advice (Chater, Huck and Inderst, 2010) (Sah, Loewenstein and Cain, 2013). However, there may still be value in requiring the disclosure of conflicts, as this can encourage advisors to avoid them altogether (Sah and Loewenstein, 2014).

Duty of care standards, which impose ethical requirements for the financial advisors to provide financial advice that is at least suitable for the client - if not requiring that it be in their best interest - are often implemented to complement disclosure requirements. These standards also typically require that the advisor take actions to minimise the conflicts they face or avoid them completely, and explain why their recommendation is appropriate. However, such requirements have sometimes proven difficult to enforce, in part because the advisors themselves are often not consciously aware that they are providing biased recommendations in their own interest (Moore, Tanlu and Bazerman, 2010). Having professional norms and a firm culture that avoids conflicts of interest may help to promote the provision of financial advice in the best interests of clients (OECD, 2016).

Where disclosure and duty of care standards have not adequately improved consumer outcomes from financial advice, policy makers have targeted the source of conflicts of interest and imposed direct limits on how financial advisors are remunerated. Several jurisdictions have banned the payment of commissions to independent financial advisors. Such measures have been shown to affect the advice provided (OECD, 2016).

Nevertheless, making the cost of advice more transparent to consumers may also lead fewer consumers receiving financial advice. Advisors may become unwilling to serve less profitable market segments, whether due to higher regulatory compliance costs or lower fees from less wealthy clients. Increased transparency may also lead to fewer consumers who are willing to pay for it. As such, efforts still need to be made to ensure that access to basic financial advice and products can be simple and affordable for financial consumers, and to educate them about the value of good quality financial advice, in order to maintain their trust in financial institutions.

Technology-based advice, such as robo-advice, has the potential to help close this advice gap and provide accessible and affordable financial advice for those who need it. Nevertheless, regulators need to ensure that the appropriate consumer protections are in place. These advice channels should not be held to lower standards than human advisors, and the appropriate risk controls and governance processes (including in relation to the underlying algorithms to ensure they are unbiased and resilient) must be in place to make sure that consumers will receive financial advice that is suitable for their needs (OECD, 2017e).

2.3.2. A spotlight on culture

Culture is closely linked to the issue of conduct. According to the fifth annual survey of conduct and culture published by Thomson Reuters in 2018, "culture, ethics and integrity" has been ranked by survey respondent as the top component of conduct risk, followed by "corporate governance, tone from the top" and "conflicts of interest". These components have consistently ranked as the top three over the last five years of the survey (Thomson Reuters, 2018).

Without seeking to attempt a definition, culture can generally be taken to cover the prevailing values, norms and behaviours that exist in any particular group. All groups, including financial institutions, have their own unique culture, reflecting a wide range of drivers relating to their size, nature and business model.

The drivers of culture in any financial institution comprise formal and informal drivers. According to an approach to measuring culture in financial services firms developed by Grant Thornton, in seeking to determine alignment with a firm's cultural value, positive or negative behavioural indicators might relate to drivers such a firms' control systems, organisational structure and power structure (formal) as well as rituals and routines, symbols and stories (informal) (Grant Thornton, 2016).

The role of compensation practices in financial institutions, in particular incentive-linked remuneration, as a driver of culture, has also been recognised as a contributing factor to the global financial crisis. At an international level, in 2009, the Financial Stability Board (FSB) developed the Principles for Sound Compensation Practices and their Implementation Standards to align compensation with prudent risk-taking particularly by significant financial institutions while not prescribing particular designs or levels of individual compensation (Financial Stability Forum, 2009).

The Principles require compensation practices in the financial industry to align employees' incentives with the long-term profitability of the firm. The Principles call for effective governance of compensation, and for compensation to be adjusted for all types of risk, to be symmetric with risk outcomes, and to be sensitive to the time horizon of risks. The Principles are intended to apply to all significant financial institutions but are especially critical for large, systemically important firms. The FSB undertakes regular monitoring of the implementation of the Principles.

In 2018, the FSB published supplementary guidance to the FSB Principles following public consultation (Financial Stability Board, 2018). The guidance provides firms and supervisors with a framework to consider how compensation practices and tools, such as in-year bonus adjustments, malus or clawback, can be used to reduce misconduct risk and address misconduct incidents.

In terms of developments in different jurisdictions, for example, the UK Financial Conduct Authority (FCA) has made culture a major priority in its supervision approach. The FCA has identified four key area of focus relating to culture: a firm's purpose, leadership, approach to rewarding and managing people and governance arrangements.

In addition to the introduction of remuneration reforms alluded to above, a key aspect of the FCA's overall approach to culture is the Senior Manager and Certification Regime, the aim of which is reduce harm to consumers and strengthen market integrity by making individuals more accountable for their conduct and competence. The Senior Manager Regime, which replaced the previous Approved Person Regime, was introduced for deposit taking institution and some investment firms in March 2016, and extended to insurance companies in December 2018.

In Australia, issues relating to remuneration, culture and governance have been at the centre of the Royal Commission into Misconduct in the Banking, Superannuation and Financial Services Industry, established in November 2017 to look into alleged misconduct of Australian banks and other financial services entities. In announcing the Royal Commission, it was noted by the then Prime Minister and Treasurer that "trust in a well-functioning banking and financial services industry promotes financial system stability, growth, efficiency and innovation over the long term" (Department of the Treasury Australia, 2017).

Measures relating to the culture within financial institutions have formed the basis of a number of recommendations to Government set out in the final report of the Royal Commission, included the extension of the Banking Executive Accountability Regime beyond banks to other regulated entities such as superannuation and insurance companies. This regime, which was introduced in September 2017, establishes accountability obligations on directors and senior executives of financial institutions, as well as deferred remuneration and notification obligations. At the same time, Australian financial services regulators have signalled they are stepping up their focus on culture.

In April 2018, the Monetary Authority of Singapore (MAS) proposed new guidelines to strengthen the individual accountability of senior managers and raise conduct within financial institution. The guidelines are a key part of MAS' broader efforts to foster a culture of ethical conduct and responsible risk-taking in the financial services industry. Similar to the emphasis in other jurisdictions, MAS has clearly highlighted the link between culture and conduct. In a speech given in March 2017, Mr Lee Boon Ngiap, Assistant Managing Director, MAS, identified the following key drivers of a positive culture within financial institutions: strong and clear tone from the top; people management and incentives; escalation policies; recruitment and training; and self-policing (Monetary Authority of Singapore, 2017). Once again, the role of incentive and culture is made clear.

In Hong Kong, China broadly similar requirements have been introduced via the Manager-in-Charge regime implemented in October 2017. Licensed corporations are expected to designate fit and proper individuals to be Managers-In-Charge of each of these functions. The Manager-in-Charge regime is part of reinforcing a culture of accountability within financial institution and ensuring clarity about who has responsibility for what. Banks conducting regulated activities, i.e. registered institutions, are also expected to identify at least one individual (expected to be Chief Executives including Alternate Chief Executives, directors approved or managers appointed under the Banking Ordinance) as principally responsible for the overall management of the institution, to the extent that these individuals are involved in the management of the business constituting any regulated activity for which the registered institution is registered.

In 2017, the Hong Kong Monetary Authority (HKMA) initiated a Bank Culture Reform through promoting the adoption of a holistic and effective framework for fostering a sound culture within authorized institutions (AIs), with particular attention given to three pillars, namely governance, incentive systems, and assessment and feedback mechanisms. Practical guidance on these three pillars was also provided to all AIs and, following consultation with the industry and drawing upon the experience from overseas practices, the HKMA announced its supervisory measures for bank culture (namely, self-assessment, focused reviews and culture dialogues) in December 2018.

Other jurisdictions around the world have also increased the focus of their attention on the responsibilities of senior staff within financial institutions in a bid to promote a culture of accountability and responsibility.

2.3.3. Quality financial products

One of the drivers (and also a consequence) of poor conduct and culture in a financial institution is an environment where financial products are not designed and distributed to meet the needs of the customers to whom they are sold, but rather financial and other incentives for selling the product are prioritised without due regard to the suitability of the product.

As noted in a 2018 speech given by James Shipton, the Chairman of the Australian Securities and Investments Commission on the topic of rebuilding trust, the first of six components of a good financial system is "financial products [that] do what they say they will do. Meaning that the design of products does not take advantage of asymmetric information, consumer biases or lack of knowledge about the product. This also means these providers have sufficient training and experience in relation to the product or service – this goes to their competence" (ASIC, 2018).

Financial consumer protection frameworks have traditionally included requirements relating to the disclosure of relevant information about financial products and services. As already noted, it is increasingly recognised that, by itself, disclosure may not provide a sufficient degree of financial consumer protection supporting good outcomes for financial consumers from the products or services they pay for. While there may be scope to enhance the effectiveness of disclosure through behavioural research or use of different channels or formats (e.g. use of digital), this reflects both the low level of engagement of many consumers with traditional disclosure documents, and the tendency of some financial service providers to disclose information in an opaque or legalistic way, designed to protect the provider rather than the customer.

This recognition has, among other things, led to a focus in a number of jurisdictions on the governance of financial products themselves, in terms of enhanced obligations relating to the manufacture and distribution of financial products. These sorts of obligations supplement requirements relating to disclosure, marketing and selling of financial products, and are focussed on the design of the product and its suitability for the target market for whom it is intended.

For example, in the European Union, MiFID II, which came into force in January 2018, introduced extensive product governance requirements on both manufacturers and distributors of investment products. Under the Directive, financial institutions that manufacture investment products are required to identify, and take reasonable steps to distribute to a target market of end clients. Distributors need to have sufficient understanding of manufacturers' products and product approval process in order to identify and sell to their own identified target market. In addition, financial institutions must ensure that staff remuneration and performance assessments are not organised in a way that goes against clients' interests. For instance, this may happen when remuneration or performance targets provide an incentive for staff to recommend a particular financial product instead of another that would better meet clients' needs.

Also in the EU, the European Banking Authority introduced Guidelines on Product Oversight & Governance in January 2017. The Guidelines deal with the establishment of product governance and oversight arrangements for both manufacturers and distributors as an integral part of the general organisational requirements linked to internal control systems of firms. They refer to internal processes, functions and strategies aimed at designing products, bringing them to the market, and reviewing them over their life cycle. They also establish procedures relevant for ensuring the interests, objectives and characteristics of the target market are met. Competent authorities across the EU are required to incorporate the Guidelines in their national frameworks or practices.

Relatedly, a review of product governance in small and medium sized bank conducted by the UK FCA identified examples of good practice, including that the most effective product governance frameworks focused on delivering good customer outcomes during all stages of the product lifecycle, from design to review. Another element of good practice was that senior management provided a positive "tone from the top". Good practice also included being active in seeking customer feedback, both for existing products and services and for new communications, via traditional means, such as customer surveys, dedicated customer panels and focus groups.

Another example is that of Australia, where new laws are proposed to introduce requirements relating to the design and distribution of financial products to ensure that products are targeted at the right people, and a temporary product intervention power for the market conduct regulator (the Australian Securities and Investments Commission) to intervene when there is a risk of significant consumer detriment. Among other things, the proposed new laws are intended to increase the accountability of product issuers and distributors, reduce the likelihood of consumers acquiring (or being mis-sold) products without fully understanding the associated risks and that are misaligned with their financial situation, objectives and needs, and, in this way, promote greater consumer confidence and trust in the system (Department of the Treasury Australia, 2016).

In the United States, the Consumer Financial Protection Bureau (CFPB) has power to intervene where conduct or practices are 'unfair, deceptive or abusive'. This can involve administrative action through cease and desist orders and legislative action through rule-making powers.

2.4. Enhancing trust in institutional investors through responsible business conduct

Edelman has identified 16 drivers of trust across business. Among these over a quarter are directly related to responsible business conduct (RBC).[2] These include: having ethical business practices; putting customers above profit, working to protect and improve the environment; addressing society's needs in its everyday business; and partnering with NGOs, government and third parties to address societal issues (Edelman, 2012).

RBC-related drivers have historically received less attention in the financial sector than in industries with more direct social and environmental footprints. However, the role of RBC for trust building in financial institutions, and particularly for institutional investors has become increasingly important in recent years.

2.4.1. Why is RBC important in driving trust of institutional investors?

Clients and beneficiaries or institutional investors are also increasingly calling on institutional investors to take environmental, social and governance (ESG) factors into account in their decision making. In the United States, 80% of asset managers cited increasing client demand as their motivation for pursuing sustainability strategies (Calvert Investments, 2015). Likewise, a study conducted amongst members of the Dutch DB pension fund found that 66.7% of participants favoured investing their pension savings in a responsible manner (Bauer, R. et al., 2018). Demand for responsible investment is especially strong amongst millennials. For example, an EY survey suggests that millennial investors are twice as likely as others to invest in companies with ESG practices. As the investment share of millennials continues to increase, demand for responsible investment can likewise be expected to continue to grow. (EY, 2017)

Furthermore a growing body of empirical evidence suggests that investments which take ESG factors into account can add value and lead to higher risk-adjusted returns net of expenses. ESG factors appear to have, at best a positive relationship with corporate financial performance and at worst a neutral relationship. (OECD, 2017a). For example, a recent study by PRI found that, in the world portfolio, ESG momentum strategies (i.e. portfolios with improving ESG scores) and tilt strategies (i.e. portfolios with high ESG scores) outperformed the MSCI World Index by 16.8% and 11.2% respectively in active cumulative returns over a 10-year period. (PRI, 2018) Similarly, a 2017 study by BofA Merrill Lynch Global Research found that stocks that ranked within the top third by ESG scores outperformed stocks in the bottom third by 18 percentage points in the 2005 to 2015 period. It also found that ESG was a better signal of future earnings volatility, relative to other fundamental factors. (PRI, 2018)

Further research would be valuable in determining whether these trends reflect short-term results or a more general, sustained pattern, as investing in new asset classes or investment opportunities where demand significantly outpaces supply can create gains that may disappear as markets converge to equilibrium overtime. In this regard strategies which take into account ESG factors should also be evaluated to assess whether they deliver better risk-adjusted returns net of costs than other investment opportunities.

Additionally, the introduction of global sustainability agendas has likely played a role in enhancing expectations of institutional investors with respect to RBC. In 2015, the Paris Agreement and the Sustainable Development Goals (SDGs) were adopted. The role of the financial sector is explicitly referenced in the Paris Agreement, which states as one of its primary objectives "[m]aking finance flows consistent with a pathway towards low greenhouse gas emissions and climate-resilient development." (United Nations, 2015) Governments are also increasingly inclined to exploit the scale of assets and leverage of financial institutions to support these global sustainability objectives. In this respect G20 leaders have highlighted the need to align financial flows (from both public and private institutions) to promote environmental goals and achieve the objectives of the SDGs. (G20, 2017).

Do current practices of institutional investors go far enough?

As the importance of RBC for trust in institutional investors is becoming increasingly significant, investors are responding to this demand. Morgan Stanley (2018) finds that 84% of surveyed asset owners are pursuing or considering pursuing ESG integration in their investment process, and 60% of them only began doing so in the last four years.

Box 2.2. Responsible investment strategies

A variety of approaches exist with respect to responsible investment. While there is no formal definition of these different approaches the below terminology has been associated with the described strategies.

Responsible Investing- often used as a catch all term that may encompass various strategies which take into account environmental and social issues in the context of investment decision making.

Environmental, Social, Governance (ESG) Integration - defined by the Principles for Responsible Investment (PRI) as "the explicit and systematic inclusion of ESG issues in investment analysis and investment decisions." ESG criteria may be used primarily to identify financial risks posed by real or potential ESG impacts.

Impact investment - products or strategies that seek to generate positive social or environmental impacts alongside a financial return.

Ethical investment – products or strategies that are dictated by certain ethical or moral considerations. For example, exclusionary or screening processes which exclude investment in certain industries (e.g. tobacco).

As a result the market for responsible investment is growing. For example, US money managers' assets under management that have incorporated ESG issues has risen from less than USD 325 billion trillion in 2008 to over USD 11 trillion last year. While the majority of this investing is from asset management entities, market-based product development for institutional and retail clients is also growing through ESG oriented mutual funds and exchange traded funds (ETFs). The market for responsible investment is currently worth approximately USD 23 trillion. (JP Morgan, 2018)

However, current strategies for responsible investment vary widely in terms of objectives, scope of application as well as prevalence of use amongst institutional investors. For example, a survey by the Alternative Investment Management Association (AIMA) of 582 institutional investors worldwide showed that out of those who reported implementing an "ESG strategy", 47% use exclusionary strategies, while only 21% practice full integration of ESG risk factors (AIMA, 2018). Moreover, many financial institutions do not have any meaningful strategy in place for responding to significant ESG risks. In this respect, a recent study of the world's 100 largest pension funds found that 60% of funds have little or no approach to environmental risks. (ShareAction, 2018)

Financial institutions continue to point to several challenges hindering their ability to meaningfully pursue responsible investment strategies. Among these challenges are: understanding and design of existing governance frameworks (OECD 2017a), poor understanding of ESG risks and lack of standardised approaches to ESG risk management (State Street Global Advisors, 2018), and lack of quality data and comparative metrics on ESG issues (Morgan Stanley, 2018).

2.4.2. How can policy makers support responsible investment to drive trust?

Policy-makers can play an instrumental role in responding to some of the above mentioned challenges, thereby facilitating responsible investment and enhancing trust.

Integrating consideration of ESG factors into governance frameworks

Research by the OECD has found that while current regulatory frameworks on investment governance do not represent a de facto barrier to responsible investment strategies many institutional investors continue to interpret them as such (OECD 2017a). This is because some investors continue to see a conflict between their responsibility to protect the financial interests of their beneficiaries and the consideration of ESG factors. It is also because most investment governance regulatory frameworks and risk-based controls generally do not explicitly refer to ESG factors, which has meant that investors and other financial institutions have had to interpret for themselves the extent to which responsible investment strategies are possible or permitted (OECD, 2017a).

Furthermore, there is currently a perceived tension between ESG objectives, which are viewed as important to long-term value creation and investment horizons which seek to maximize shareholder value in the short term. In a survey by State Street, 47% of asset owners and 43% of asset managers indicated that they believe that the proper timeframe for expecting responsible investment strategies to deliver outperformance is five years or more, but only 10%-20% use these time frames for evaluating performance. Investment performance is still generally measured and reported on 1-, 3- and 5-year time horizons. (Michael T. Cappucci, 2017) The importance of long-term oriented strategies for building trust and stability has been emphasised by the CEO of Blackrock, the world's largest asset manager, in his letters to CEOs of companies invested in by Blackrock. (Fink, 2018 and 2019)

In recent years, policy makers have taken steps through regulation and other instruments to explicitly recognise the importance of taking into account long-term value drivers such as environmental and social risks in investment governance (Sullivan, R. et al., 2015).

For example, in several countries, investors are being asked to consider ESG factors as part of investor stewardship activities. In the UK, the Financial Reporting Council (FRC) will update in 2019 the Stewardship Code which already refers to ESG factors (Financial Reporting Council, 2019). In Japan, a Council of Experts revised in 2017 the Stewardship Code (2014), with explicit references to risks arising from ESG factors (Financial Services Agency, 2019). Likewise, the Code for Responsible Investment in South Africa provides guidelines for institutional investors on integrating ESG factors in investment processes.

Some countries have included duties related to sustainability in corporate governance codes. For example, the 2015 German Corporate Governance Code was amended in 2017 to include a reference to sustainability for institutional investors noting "[i]nstitutional investors […] are expected to exercise their ownership rights actively and responsibly, in accordance with transparent principles that also respect the concept of sustainability" (Regierungskommission, 2017). Clarifying duties with respect to environmental and social issues is also a key action point under the EU Sustainable Finance Action Plan, which notes that "[…] the Commission will table a legislative proposal to clarify institutional investors' and asset managers' duties in relation to sustainability considerations […]. The proposal will aim to (i) explicitly require institutional investors and asset managers to integrate sustainability considerations in the investment decision-making process […].". (EU, 2018)

Introducing clear mandates for inclusion of ESG factors into decision making of financial institutions through policy or regulation will be helpful to encouraging financial institutions to do so. However, policy makers should also develop coherent investor governance frameworks, performance reporting and investment planning which is compatible with ESG objectives.

Promoting common and widespread expectations

A lack of common expectations is also an obstacle to more widespread adoption of responsible investment strategies by institutional investors. A survey conducted in 2016-2017 with investment executives at 475 institutions found that over half of institutional investors implementing some form of responsible investment strategy felt there was a lack of clarity around standards and terminology (State Street Global Advisors, 2018). A lack of standardisation allows investors broad flexibility to design and implement their own approaches. However, this ambiguity also creates challenges to benchmarking performance with respect to environmental and social factors and heightens the risk of "green-washing", which can diminish the credibility of responsible investment strategies and their potential for trust-building.

Developing and recognising common standards with respect to responsible investment can promote quality processes and enhance its potential for trust building. It could also provide a common reference point or baseline of expectations for institutional investors and mitigate the risk of a multiplication of varying expectations across jurisdictions and initiatives.

In this respect the OECD due diligence framework may serve as reference points for policy makers. In 2017, the OECD articulated key considerations for institutional investors in carrying out due diligence to identify and respond to environmental and social risks, within their portfolios. This publication was developed with the support of leading asset owners and investment managers and has been formally endorsed by 48 governments (OECD, 2017). The European Union recently reached agreement on an EU Regulation for Sustainable Investor Disclosure. Once implemented, this regulation will call on financial market participants and financial advisors to integrate consideration of ESG risks and opportunities in their processes and to report on their due diligence policies. The regulation also encourages financial market participants to take into account due diligence guidance for responsible business conduct developed by the OECD (OECD, 2018e).

By promoting common expectations on responsible investment, policy makers can help to level the playing field and encourage industry laggards to perform better. In this respect, policy makers can build on and promote existing recognised standards to foster a common understanding of responsible investment.

Improving disclosure and generating data quality

A lack of quality data has been raised as a central challenge by institutional investors in both pursuing responsible investment strategies and measuring the financial performance of such strategies. For example, 68% of asset owners surveyed in a Morgan Stanley study noted that a lack of availability of quality ESG data is the leading challenge to responsible investment. (Morgan Stanley, 2018)

Challenges associated with data are based both on availability of information and quality of data. For example, a 2014 report by the Sustainable Stock Exchange Initiative estimates that only 5 000-10 000 out of the 80 000 multinational companies in the world publish environmental and social performance reports. (Sustainable Stock Exchange Initative, 2014)

In an effort to respond to this gap, increased regulation on sustainability reporting has been on the rise. A 2015 study by KPMG estimates that 41% of countries examined had some form of mandatory social reporting (KPMG, 2015). At the EU level, a non-financial disclosure directive was introduced in 2014 which requires reporting on environmental impacts and human rights as well as due diligence processes, for large, publically listed companies, including financial institutions (EU, 2014). France has introduced reporting requirement specific to investors. Article 173-VI of the Energy Transition Act for Green Growth requires asset owners and investment managers to disclose climate-related financial risks and report on how ESG criteria are considered in their investment decisions (Legifrance, 2015).

While efforts to encourage sustainability reporting are accelerating, reporting requirements are usually voluntary ("comply or explain") and are not prescriptive on the methods or metrics to be used in measuring or reporting on ESG issues. As a result the reported information may not be useful for end users. For example, an EY analysis of reports filed in response to Article 173-VI of the Energy Transition Act found that while "investors disclosed metrics linking investees' GHG emissions to key financial indicators and assessing alignment of these emissions with a 2°C scenario ...[m]ethodological limitations make any comparison of these metrics impossible" (EY, 2017).

Challenges with data quality and reporting are even greater when it comes to tracking and reporting social issues. One primary challenge is translating qualitative indicators normally associated with social risks into quantitative metrics. Another is the lack of standardised social benchmarks. For example, research by the NYU Stern school finds no consistent set of standards defining the "S" in ESG frameworks and that most frameworks measure social issues vaguely or with respect to just a small set of labour concerns (O'Connor C. and Labowitz, S., 2017).

Policy makers can play an important role in promoting higher quality reporting and data through scaling up efforts for reporting standardisation and impact measurements. As part of its implementation of the Sustainable Finance Action Plan, the EU has emphasised the importance of facilitating quality data and benchmarking. For example, key components of the Action Plan include: establishing an EU classification system for sustainable activities (Action 1); creating standards and labels for green financial products (Action 2) developing and harmonising sustainability benchmarks related to carbon (Action 5) and strengthening sustainability disclosure and accounting rule-making (Action 9). As part of the Action Plan, the EU is currently developing a taxonomy to reflect commonly agreed principles and metrics for assessing whether economic activities can be considered environmentally sustainable for investment purposes.

Expanding such initiatives beyond environmental risks and ensuring coherence across jurisdiction will be important to responding to existing gaps in ESG data for institutional investors.

2.5. Conclusion

In the wake of the financial crisis, significant reforms were introduced to prevent against future crises as well as rebuild trust in the financial sector. While these initiatives have been helpful in regaining public trust, additional work is necessary to respond to new and ongoing challenges as well as increasing expectations of beneficiaries and society more broadly of the financial sector.

This chapter addresses three areas essential to understanding and strengthening people's lack of trust in financial institutions. The section on pensions highlights the importance of pension governance and transparency, financial literacy, the alignment of fees and costs, and ESG investment to improve trust in pensions. The section on financial consumer protection focuses on managing potential conflicts of interest, culture and quality of products. The section on responsible business conduct concentrates on governance, standard setting, data and disclosure. More work is required in all three areas to improve people's trust in financial institutions.

With respect to pensions and pension funds, several activities could be useful in enhancing trust including:

- Better communication regarding the features of the pension system, the purpose of different reforms, and adjustments to the system.
- Further improvements in the design of DC pension plans accounting for behavioural biases and low financial knowledge.

Additionally, the regulatory framework needs to be strengthened further by making sure that pension funds work in the best interest of members. In this respect:

- The independence and, the internal and external, oversight of pension funds' governing body need further strengthening in many jurisdictions.
- The supervision and monitoring of pension funds also needs to improve further, as well as data disclosure and standardisation, especially on the costs of providing services to members.
- There is still a lot to do on the fees charged by pension funds making sure that they are aligned with the actual costs for pension funds of managing people's retirement. Some of the ideas are discussed in the chapter and in other OECD reports (OECD, 2018b).

In terms of promoting trust and confidence via financial consumer protection policies, the application of robust conduct regulation, disclosure and other activities, needs to be reinforced by considering more qualitative factors such as:

- Ensuring financial institutions have the appropriate culture in terms of safeguarding and prioritising customers' interests and ensuring the quality and value of the financial products and services on offer.

The role of RBC in trust building for institutional investors can only be expected to become more significant in the coming years as millennials' share of global investment grows and the impacts (both financial and real) of environmental risks and irresponsible business practices are felt more acutely. While there has been increased interest and efforts by institutional investors to take environmental and social issues into account in their activities, to date the level of ambition and approaches of institutional investors have varied considerably but have largely been limited in scope.

As investors seek to respond to increasing demand for responsible investment they will have to enhance existing approaches. Policy makers can facilitate institutional investors in this respect in several ways:

- Supporting investment governance frameworks that are compatible with and support ESG objectives.
- Fostering common and widespread expectations with respect to responsible investment, for example due diligence processes for responsible business conduct.
- Supporting efforts to promote quality ESG data and disclosures.

Some governments have already initiated such efforts. Scaling up these efforts and ensuring coherence across approaches will be important to enhancing trust in this sector amongst consumers, beneficiaries and society more broadly.

Notes

[1] For the purposes of this chapter, financial institutions refer to private, commercial institutions involved in investment, advisory, insurance, finance, or retail banking services for clients. Public institutions such as central banks, development finance institutions or government-run export credit agencies and intermediary service providers such as credit risk agencies and market research providers are not included.

[2] The OECD defines responsible business conduct (RBC) as: a) making a positive contribution to economic, environmental and social progress with a view to achieving sustainable development; and b) avoiding and addressing adverse impacts related to an enterprise's direct and indirect operations, products or services. The OECD articulates what constitutes RBC through the OECD Guidelines for Multinational Enterprises (OECD, 2011b), a comprehensive set of government-backed recommendations on RBC.

References

Act no. 2017-399 of 27 March 2017 published in OJ no. 0074 of 28 March 2017 www.legifrance.gouv.fr/eli/loi/2017/3/27/2017-399/jo/texte.

AIMA (2018), "ESG Integration on the Rise: And how to implement it in your portfolio", www.aima.org/journal/aima-journal-edition-114/article/esg-integration-on-the-rise-and-how-to-implement-it-in-your-portfolio.html.

Atkinson, A. and F. Messy (2012), "Measuring Financial Literacy: Results of the OECD / International Network on Financial Education (INFE) Pilot Study", *OECD Working Papers on Finance, Insurance and Private Pensions*, No. 15, OECD Publishing, Paris, https://dx.doi.org/10.1787/5k9csfs90fr4-en.

ACSI (2018), *Australian Asset Owner Stewardship Code*, Australian Council of Superannuation Investors, www.acsi.org.au/publications-1/australian-asset-owner-stewarship-code.html.

Australian Securities and Investments Commission (2018), "Rebuilding trust: A conduct regulator's perspective", Regulatory address by James Shipton, Chair, Australian Securities and Investments Commission, https://download.asic.gov.au/media/4691647/james-shipton-afr-banking-and-wealth-summit-speech-5-april-2018.pdf.

Bank of America Corporation (2018), *U.S. Trust Insights on Wealth and Worth*, https://newsroom.bankofamerica.com/system/files/2018_US_Trust_Insights_on_Wealth_and_Worth_Overview.pdf.

Banks, J. and Z. Oldfield (2007), "Understanding pensions: Cognitive function, numerical ability and retirement saving", *Fiscal Studies*, Vol. 28, No. 2, pp. 143-170.

Barrett, A., I. Mosca and B.J. Whelan (2013), "(Lack of) pension knowledge", IZA Discussion Paper, No. 7596, August 2013, www.iza.org/en/webcontent/publications/papers/viewAbstract?dp_id=7596.

Bauer, R. and T. Ruof, and P. Smeets (2018), *Get Real! Individuals Prefer More Sustainable Investments*, available at http://dx.doi.org/10.2139/ssrn.3287430.

Business and Human Rights Centre (2017), *Netherlands: Parliament adopts child labour due diligence law for companies; Senate approval pending*, www.business-humanrights.org/en/netherlands-parliament-adopts-child-labour-due-diligence-law-for-companies-senate-approval-pending.

Calvert Investments (2015), *Perspectives on ESG Integration in Equity Investing: An opportunity to enhance long-term, risk-adjusted investment performance*, www.sustainablefinance.ch/upload/cms/user/201507_Calvert_PerspectivesOnESGIntegrationInEquityInvesting.pdf.

Cappucci, M. T. (2017), "The ESG Integration Paradox", Harvard Management Company, https://corpgov.law.harvard.edu/2017/07/26/the-esg-integration-paradox/.

Chater, N., S. Huck and R. Inderst (2010), "Consumer Decision-Making in Retail Investment Services: A Behavioural Economics Perspective – Final Report".

Consumers International (2017), *Building a Digital World Consumers Can Trust,* www.consumersinternational.org/media/1822/ci-summary_english_updated.pdf.

Department of the Treasury Australia (2017), *Royal Commission – Banks and Financial Services*, http://sjm.ministers.treasury.gov.au/media-release/124-2017/.

Department of the Treasury Australia (2016), *Design and distribution obligations and product intervention power*, https://treasury.gov.au/consultation/design-and-distribution-obligations-and-product-intervention-power.

Dushi, I. and H.M. Iams (2010), "The impact of response error on participation rates and contributions to defined contribution pension plans", *Social Security Bulletin*, Vol. 70, No. 1, www.socialsecurity.gov/policy/docs/ssb/v70n1/v70n1p45.pdf

Edelman (2018), *2018 Edelman Trust Barometer*, www.edelman.com/research/2018-edelman-trust-barometer.

Edelman (2017), *Trust Barometer – Financial Services Results*, www.slideshare.net/EdelmanInsights/2017-edelman-trust-barometer-financial-services-results

Edelman (2015), *2015 Edelman Trust Barometer – Global Results*, www.slideshare.net/EdelmanInsights/2015-edelman-trust-barometer-global-results/31-BUILDINGTRUST.

Edelman (2012), *2012 Edelman Trust Barometer*, www.edelman.com/research/2012-edelman-trust-barometer.

Edelman (2009), *2009 Edelman Trust Barometer,* www.edelman.com/sites/g/files/aatuss191/files/2018-10/2009-Trust-Barometer-Global-Deck.pdf.

Equator Principles (2019), *EP Association Members & Reporting*, https://equator-principles.com/members-reporting/ (accessed 14 January 2019).

Equator Principles (2013), *The Equator Principles*, https://equator-principles.com/wp-content/uploads/2017/03/equator_principles_III.pdf.

European Banking Authority, *Guidelines on product oversight and governance arrangements for retail banking products,* https://eba.europa.eu/documents/10180/1141044/EBA-GL-2015-18+Guidelines+on+product+oversight+and+governance.pdf.

EU (2018), Communication from the Commission to the European Parliament, the European Council, The Council, The European Central Bank, The European Economic and Social Committee and the

Committee of the Regions Action Plan: Financing Sustainable Growth, https://eur-lex.europa.eu/legal-content/EN/TXT/?uri=CELEX:52018DC0097.

EU (2014), Directive 2014/95/EU of the European Parliament and of the Council of 22 October 2014 amending Directive 2013/34/EU as regards disclosure of non-financial and diversity information by certain large undertakings and groups, http://data.europa.eu/eli/dir/2014/95/oj.

EY (2017a), *Sustainable Investing: the millennial investor*, www.ey.com/Publication/vwLUAssets/ey-sustainable-investing-the-millennial-investor-gl/$FILE/ey-sustainable-investing-the-millennial-investor.pdf.

EY (2017b), *How have investors met their ESG and climate reporting requirements under Article 173-VI?*, www.ey.com/Publication/vwLUAssets/ey-how-have-investors-met-their-esg-and-climate-reporting-requirements-under-article-173-vi/$FILE/ey-how-have-investors-met-their-esg-and-climate-reporting-requirements-under-article-173-vi.pdf.

Federal Government (2017), *National Action Plan Implementation of the UN Guiding Principles on Business and Human Rights*, www.auswaertiges-amt.de/blob/610714/fb740510e8c2fa83dc507afad0b2d7ad/nap-wirtschaft-menschenrechte-engl-data.pdf.

Financial Conduct Authority (2018), "Retail banking: product governance review", www.fca.org.uk/publications/multi-firm-reviews/retail-banking-product-governance-review (accessed 22 January 2019).

Financial Reporting Council (2019), *UK Stewardship Code*, www.frc.org.uk/investors/uk-stewardship-code (accessed 14 January 2019).

Financial Services Agency (2019), *The Council of Experts on the Stewardship Code*, www.fsa.go.jp/en/refer/councils/stewardship/index.html (accessed 14 January 2019).

Financial Stability Forum (2009), *FSF Principles for Sound Compensation Practices*, https://www.fsb.org/wp-content/uploads/r_0904b.pdf.

Financial Stability Board (2018), *Supplementary Guidance to the FSB Principles and Standards on Sound Compensation Practices*, www.fsb.org/2018/03/supplementary-guidance-to-the-fsb-principles-and-standards-on-sound-compensation-practices-2/.

Fink, L. (2019), 2019 Letter to CEOs: Purpose & Profit, www.blackrock.com/corporate/investor-relations/larry-fink-ceo-letter.

Fink, L. (2018), 2018 Letter to CEOs: A Sense of Purpose, www.blackrock.com/corporate/investor-relations/2018-larry-fink-ceo-letter.

Fredericks, F. C. et al. (2018), *Social Cost and Material Loss: The Dakota Access Pipeline*, www.colorado.edu/project/fpiep/sites/default/files/attached-files/social_cost_and_material_loss.pdf.

Friede, G., T. Buschi and Bassen, A. (2015), "ESG and financial performance: aggregated evidence from more than 2000 empirical studies," Journal of Sustainable Finance & Investment, 5:4, 210-233, DOI: https://doi.org/10.1080/20430795.2015.1118917.

G20 (2017), *G20 Hamburg Climate and Energy Action Plan for Growth*, http://unepinquiry.org/wp-content/uploads/2017/07/Climate_and_Energy_Action_Plan_for_Growth.pdf.

G20 Global Partnership on Financial Inclusion (2016), *G20 High-Level Principles for Digital Financial Inclusion*, www.gpfi.org/publications/g20-high-level-principles-digital-financial-inclusion.

Grahovar, M. (2010), *The Role of Corporate social disclosure -Trust, reputation or fashion tool?*, https://gupea.ub.gu.se/handle/2077/30501.

Grant Thornton (2016), *Measurement of culture in financial services firms*, www.grantthornton.co.uk/globalassets/1.-member-firms/united-kingdom/pdf/publication/2016/measuring-culture-in-financial-services.pdf.

Gustman, A. and T. Steinmeier (2004), "What people don't know about their pensions and social security", in W. Gale, J. Shoven and M. Warshawsky (eds.), Private Pensions and Public Policies, Brookings Institution, Washington, DC, pp. 57-125.

Gustman, A. and T. Steinmeier (1989), "An analysis of pension benefit formulas, pension wealth and incentives from pensions", Research in Labor Economics, Vol. 10, pp. 53-106.

Gustman, A., T. Steinmeier and N. Tabatabai (2008), "Do workers know about their pensions? Comparing workers' and employers' pension information," in A. Lusardi (ed.), Overcoming the Saving Slump: How to Increase the Effectiveness of Financial Education and Saving Programs, University of Chicago Press, Chicago, IL.

ILC-UK (2015), Making the system fit for purpose. London, UK, www.ilcuk.org.uk/index.php/publications/publication_details/making_the_system_fit_for_purpose.

Initiative Parlementaire 17.498 of 13 November 2017, Contre-projet indirect à l'initiative populaire "Entreprises responsables-pour protéger l'être humain et l'environnement" www.parlament.ch/en/ratsbetrieb/suche-curia-vista/geschaeft?AffairId=20170498.

Ipsos MORI (2014), *Poll Conducted for EIRIS – Ethical Finance*, www.ipsos.com/sites/default/files/migrations/en-uk/files/Assets/Docs/EIRIS%20Ethical%20Finance%20%20Investment%20toplines.pdf.

JP Morgan (2018), Sustainable Investment is Moving, https://www.jpmorgan.com/global/research/esg.

KPMG (2015), Carrots and Sticks: Global Trends in Sustainability Regulation and Policy, https://home.kpmg/content/dam/kpmg/pdf/2015/12/KPMG-survey-of-CR-reporting-2015.pdf.

Legifrance (2015), Legislative text of article 173-VI,, www.legifrance.gouv.fr/eli/loi/2015/8/17/DEVX1413992L/jo/article_173/.

Lusardi, A. and O. Mitchell (2014), "The Economic Importance of Financial Literacy: Theory and Evidence", *Journal of Economic Literature*, Vol. 52/1, http://dx.doi.org/10.1257/jel.52.1.5.

Lusardi A. and O.S. Mitchell (2011), "Financial literacy and planning: Implications for retirement wellbeing", *National Bureau of Economic Research Working Paper*, No. 17078, Cambridge, MA, www.nber.org/papers/w17078.pdf.

Mitchell, O. (1988), "Worker knowledge of pensions provisions", *Journal of Labor Economics*, Vol. 6, pp. 21-39.

Monetary Authority of Singapore (2017), *Culture and Conduct - A Regulatory Perspective - Speech by Mr Lee Boon Ngiap*, www.mas.gov.sg/News-and-Publications/Speeches-and-Monetary-Policy-Statements/Speeches/2017/Culture-and-Conduct.aspx.

Money and Pensions Panel (2013), "Basic pension: The default option for labour-market pensions", Report by the Committee of the Money and Pension Panel, www.raadtilpenge.dk/~/media/PPP/Pensionsrapport/Basic%20pension_full%20report.ashx.

Moore, D., L. Tanlu and M. Bazerman (2010), "Conflict of interest and the intrusion of bias", *Judgment and Decision Making*, Vol. 5/1, pp. 37-53.

Morgan Stanley (2018), *Sustainable Signals*, www.morganstanley.com/assets/pdfs/sustainable-signals-asset-owners-2018-survey.pdf.

O'Connell, A. (2010), "How long do we expect to live? A review of the evidence", *Journal of Population Ageing*, Vol. 4, pp. 185-201, http://link.springer.com/article/10.1007%2Fs12062-011-9049-1

O'Connor C. and S. Labowitz, (2017), *Putting the "S" in ESG: Measuring Human Rights Performance for Investors*, https://static1.squarespace.com/static/547df270e4b0ba184dfc490e/t/58cad912e58c6274180b58b6/1489688854754/Metrics-Report-final-1.pdf.

OECD (2018a), *Financial Incentives and Retirement Savings*, OECD Publishing, Paris, https://doi.org/10.1787/9789264306929-en.

OECD (2018b), *OECD Pensions Outlook 2018*, OECD Publishing, Paris, https://doi.org/10.1787/pens_outlook-2018-en.

OECD (2018c), *G20/OECD Policy Guidance on Digitalisation and Financial Literacy,* www.oecd.org/finance/G20-OECD-INFE-Policy-Guidance-Digitalisation-Financial-Literacy-2018.pdf.

OECD (2018d), *G20/OECD Policy Guidance Financial Consumer Protection Approaches in the Digital Age,* www.oecd.org/finance/G20-OECD-Policy-Guidance-Financial-Consumer-Protection-Digital-Age-2018.pdf.

OECD (2018e), OECD Due Diligence Guidance for Responsible Business Conduct, http://mneguidelines.oecd.org/due-diligence-guidance-for-responsible-business-conduct.htm.

OECD (2017a), *Investment Governance and the Integration of Environmental, Social and Governance Factors*, www.oecd.org/finance/Investment-Governance-Integration-ESG-Factors.pdf.

OECD (2017b), *OECD Guidelines on Measuring Trust*, OECD Publishing, Paris, https://doi.org/10.1787/9789264278219-en.

OECD (2017c), *Responsible business conduct for institutional investors: Key considerations for due diligence under the OECD Guidelines for Multinational Enterprises*, https://mneguidelines.oecd.org/RBC-for-Institutional-Investors.pdf.

OECD (2017d), *Investing in Climate: Investing in Growth,* OECD Publishing, Paris, www.oecd.org/environment/investing-in-climate-investing-in-growth-9789264273528-en.htm.

OECD (2017e), *Robo-advice for Pensions,* www.oecd.org/pensions/Robo-Advice-for-Pensions-2017.pdf.

OECD (2016a), *OECD Pensions Outlook 2016*, OECD Publishing, Paris, https://doi.org/10.1787/23137649.

OECD (2016b), "Policy measures to improve the quality of financial advice for retirement", in *OECD Pensions Outlook 2016*, OECD Publishing, Paris, https://doi.org/10.1787/pens_outlook-2016-6-en.

OECD (2016c), "The role of financial education in supporting decision-making for retirement", in *OECD Pensions Outlook 2016*, OECD Publishing, Paris, https://doi.org/10.1787/pens_outlook-2016-8-en.

OECD (2016d), OECD Core Principles of Private Pension Regulation, www.oecd.org/pensions/principles-private-pension-regulation.htm.

OECD (2015), *G20/OECD Principles of Corporate Governance*, OECD Publishing, Paris, https://doi.org/10.1787/9789264236882-en.

OECD (2012a), OECD roadmap for the good design of defined contribution pension plans, www.oecd.org/daf/fin/private-pensions/50582753.pdf.

OECD (2012b), OECD/INFE High Level Principles on National Strategies for Financial Education, www.oecd.org/finance/financial-education/OECD-INFE-Principles-National-Strategies-Financial-Education.pdf.

OECD (2011a), G20 High Level Principles on Financial Consumer Protection, www.oecd.org/finance/financial-markets/48892010.pdf.

OECD (2011b), *OECD Guidelines for Multinational Enterprises*, http://dx.doi.org/10.1787/9789264115415-en.

PRI (2018), *Financial Performance of ESG Integration in US Investing*, www.unpri.org/download?ac=4218.

PRI (2019), *What are the Principles for Responsible Investment?*, www.unpri.org/pri/what-are-the-principles-for-responsible-investment.

PwC (2014), *How financial services lost its mojo – and how it can get it back*, https://pwc.blogs.com/files/how-financial-services-lost-its-mojo---and-how-it-can-get-it-back_full-report.pdf.

Regierundskommission (2017), German Corporate Governance Code, www.dcgk.de/files/dcgk/usercontent/en/download/code/170214_Code_markup.pdf.

Sah, S. and G. Loewenstein (2014), "Nothing to Declare: Mandatory and Voluntary Disclosure Leads Advisors to Avoid Conflicts of Interest", Psychological Science, Vol. 25/2, pp. 575-584, http://dx.doi.org/10.1177/0956797613511824.

Sah, S., G. Loewenstein and D. Cain (2013), "The burden of disclosure: Increased compliance with distrusted advice", *Journal of Personality and Social Psychology*, Vol. 104/2, pp. 289-304, http://dx.doi.org/10.1037/a0030527.

ShareAction (2018), "Pensions in a Changing Climate", https://aodproject.net/wp-content/uploads/2019/01/AODP-PensionsChangingClimate.pdf.

Sustainable Stock Exchange Initiative (2018), Progress report 2018, www.sseinitiative.org/wp-content/uploads/2018/10/SSE_On_Progress_Report_FINAL.pdf.

Sustainable Stock Exchange Initiative (2014), Progress Report 2014.

State Street Global Advisors (2018), *ESG Institutional Investor Survey*, www.ssga.com/investment-topics/environmental-social-governance/2018/04/esg-institutional-investor-survey.pdf.

Sullivan, R. et al. (2015), "Fiduciary Duty in the 21st Century", www.unpri.org/download?ac=1378.

TCFD (2017), "Recommendations of the Task Force on Climate-related Financial Disclosures", www.fsb-tcfd.org/wp-content/uploads/2017/06/FINAL-TCFD-Report-062817.pdf.

Thomson Reuters (2018), *Culture and Conduct Risk 2018*, https://legal.thomsonreuters.com/en/insights/reports/culture-and-conduct-risk-2018.

United Nations (2015), Paris Agreement, https://unfccc.int/sites/default/files/english_paris_agreement.pdf.

UN General Assembly (2018), *Working Group on the issue of human rights and transnational corporations and other business enterprises*, A/73/163, https://documents-dds-ny.un.org/doc/UNDOC/GEN/N18/224/87/PDF/N1822487.pdf?OpenElement.

UNEP FI (2018), *Principles for Responsible Banking*, www.unepfi.org/banking/bankingprinciples/.

Chapter 3. Trust and corporate liability

A key pillar of trust in business is the belief that companies conduct their operations —at a minimum—in compliance with the law. This chapter investigates this premise and finds that companies will be more likely to prevent crime and to cooperate in the detection and resolution of cases if the law provides compelling incentives for them to do so. Legal systems change slowly but Parties to the Anti-Bribery Convention have made significant progress over the last 20 years in creating such incentives and are continuing to build the legal frameworks needed to enforce laws covering economic crime.

The statistical data for Israel are supplied by and under the responsibility of the relevant Israeli authorities. The use of such data by the OECD is without prejudice to the status of the Golan Heights, East Jerusalem and Israeli settlements in the West Bank under the terms of international law.

3.1. Can companies be trusted to obey the law?

A key pillar of trust in the rule of law is the belief that businesses will strive to conduct their operations in ways that comply with the law. The building of this kind of trust takes place in two, related spheres of action. First, companies need to take appropriate steps to prevent unlawful activity from occurring within their operations. Second, once suspicions have arisen that unlawful activities have taken place, companies can report these suspicions to law enforcement authorities and cooperate in the investigation and resolution of the case (determining what happened, who was responsible and agreeing on appropriate sanctions). This degree of co-operation with law enforcement may sound unrealistic, but it does in fact occur – as discussed below, OECD data show that almost a quarter of sanctioned foreign bribery cases with known detection sources involved self-reporting by companies.[1]

3.2. Establishing a solid basis for trust

Enforcement experience relating to corporate crime suggests that trusting in companies to comply with the law should not be automatic. While companies can do much good, they can also do much harm. A company can become a nexus of criminality if it has poorly designed and implemented management systems for coordinating the activities of its employees and business partners[2]. Setting up management systems to counter the risks of criminal activity can help both prevent and detect corporate crime. The government can promote the adoption of such management systems and, more broadly, law-abiding behaviours by building in appropriate incentives, including by expanding and refining corporate liability laws to encourage compliance with law and co-operation with law enforcement.

The idea is for law enforcement authorities to tap into the comparative advantage of companies in detecting crime and contributing to investigations. To do this, corporate liability systems need to be complex enough to provide incentives for prevention, but also for constructive co-operation with law enforcement when suspicions of unlawful behaviour arise. Policy makers must also take steps to ensure that the corporate liability system is transparent and predictable for all parties potentially affected by it and that law enforcement authorities appropriately assume their roles in the law enforcement system. This is a subtle mix, one that countries are still trying to achieve.

This approach to corporate liability recognises that companies can be valuable participants when cooperating with law enforcement authorities because they know more about what happens in their operations than external investigators ever could. As will be discussed below, almost a third of countries Party to the Anti-Bribery Convention now have policies that create incentives for crime detection and prevention, as well as for self-reporting and co-operation with law enforcement authorities. With such policies in place, societies have more compelling reasons to trust business to make genuine efforts to comply with law and to contribute constructively to the law enforcement process.

3.3. Self-reporting by companies – a reliable source of detection

OECD data indicate that self-reporting by companies is, numerically, the most important single source of detection for the crime of foreign bribery. As noted earlier, OECD (2017a) shows that, while the detection source is still unknown for 55% of the foreign bribery schemes covered in the study, self-reporting played a role in almost a quarter of sanctioned foreign bribery cases, (see Figure 3.1).

Figure 3.1. How are concluded foreign bribery schemes detected: 1999-2017

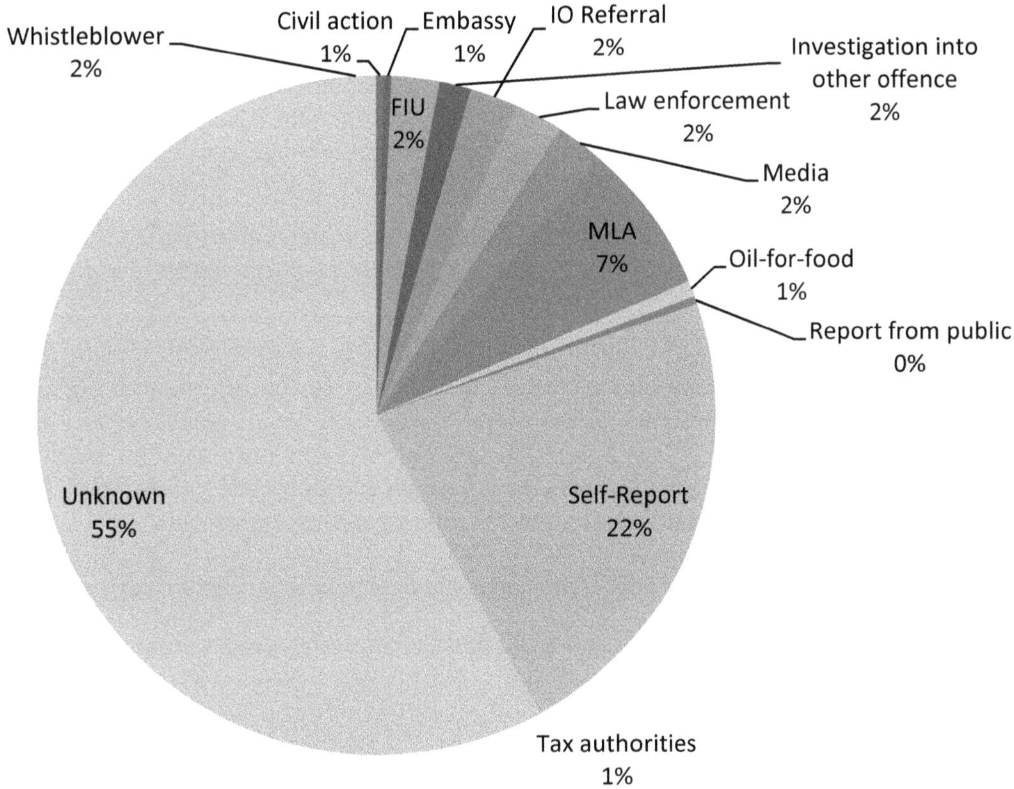

Note: Percentages have been rounded to the nearest decimal point which explains why one of the entries registers 0%. FIU = Financial Intelligence Unit. IO = International Organisation.
Source: OECD (2017a), The Detection of Foreign Bribery, page 10.

In law enforcement, case development begins with detection – that is, law enforcement authorities become aware of suspicions of criminal activity which they then pursue through investigation, prosecution and resolution in courts or by agreement with the accused. Obviously, law enforcement officials do not go to the expense and trouble of developing cases in order to have these cases dropped at the investigation or prosecution stages or to end with a 'not guilty' finding in court. Efficient law enforcement requires that enforcement authorities pursue cases that have a reasonable chance of ending with sanctions for unlawful activity or other reasonable resolutions that will stop the behaviour and reduce recidivism. Having reliable sources for the detection of crimes is important if law enforcement authorities are to zero in on such cases.

Generally, companies covered by the detection study obtained the information they self-reported from a variety of internal control processes that they use in the broader conduct of business. The most important of these is the internal audit function, which generated the information in 24% of the self-reported cases. 'Mergers and acquisitions due diligence' accounts for 7% of the self-reported cases, whistleblowers reporting to internal processes for 5% and pre-listing due diligence for 4% (OECD, 2017a, page 8).

In any case, OECD data show that self-reporting is a highly reliable source of detection. In particular, cases that were originally detected through corporate self-reporting have a higher 'yield' in terms of sanctions than the other sources of detection (such as the media or whistleblowers).

The OECD data used to show this consists of a sample of 65 concluded foreign bribery cases for which detection sources are known. These cases were resolved in one of three ways: with dropped investigations; with an acquittal or dropping at the prosecution stage; or with sanctions being imposed on individuals, companies or both. Cross tabulations between the detection sources and the sanctions allow the comparison of sanctions rates for the various sources of detection. Figure 3.2 shows that 100% of the cases that were detected through self-reporting by companies led to sanctions on companies, individuals or both.

Another relatively reliable source of detection is information provided by 'other government agencies' (which, in this sample, mainly refers to tax authorities[3]). This source of detection led to sanctions in 65% of the cases. Media and whistleblowers produced sanctions rates of 25% and 20%, respectively.

This finding of a high sanctions 'yield' from self-reporting by companies is not surprising. As noted above, there are compelling reasons to believe that the information generated from companies' internal processes offers more reliable sources of detection than other sources. The challenge for policy makers in law enforcement is to develop incentives systems that motivate companies to divulge accurate and complete information about wrongdoing that they suspect has occurred in the context of their operations.

Figure 3.2. Sanctions 'yield' of different sources of detection in foreign bribery cases

(Percentage of cases that ended in at least one sanction, out of 65 foreign bribery cases)

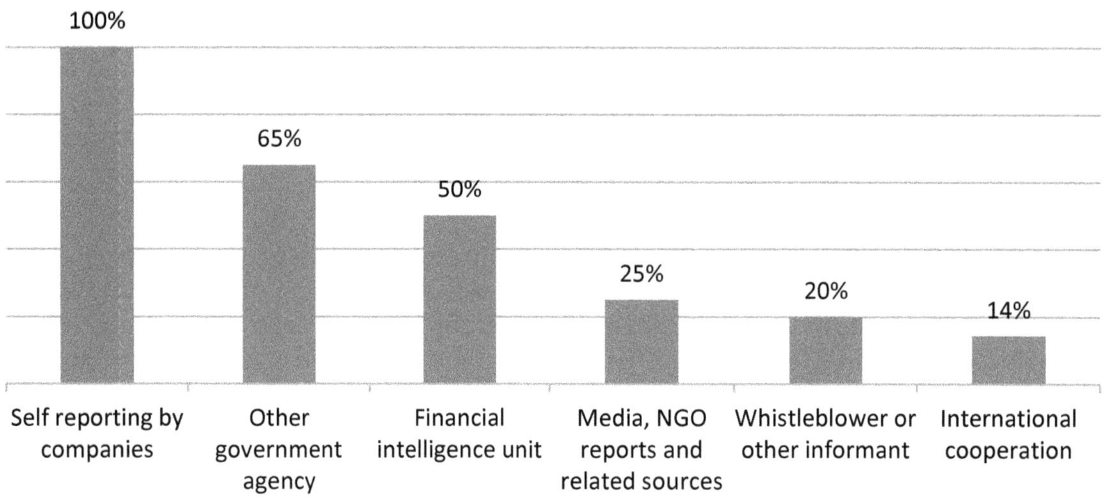

Note: In 9 cases, the source of detection was self-reporting – all 9 ended in at least one sanction on an individual or a company. The numbers of other cases from other detections sources include the following: 20 cases where the source was another government agency in the same country; 6 cases of Financial Intelligence Units providing information mainly from suspicious transactions reports; 14 cases involving mutual legal assistance or other international information sharing among law enforcement authorities; 8 cases of media investigations or NGO reports. In 10 of the cases, there were 2 sources. The cross-tabulation with sanctions for these 10 cases attributes a 'sanctions outcome' to both of the sources for these cases.

Source: Information submitted by members of the OECD Working Group on Bribery in the context of Working Group monitoring of members' observance of their obligations under the Anti-Bribery Convention. Data on concluded cases for which detection sources are known is available for the following countries: Denmark (4 cases from the Phase 3 Follow-up monitoring process); Finland (7 cases from the Phase 4 monitoring process), Germany (41 cases from the Phase 4 monitoring process), Israel (5 cases from the Phase 3 Follow-up process) and Norway (8 cases from the Phase 4 monitoring process).

It is important to stress that the data also suggest that detection sources interact and are possibly mutually reinforcing – in 10 of the 65 cases, there was more than one source of detection. Thus, information provided by other government agencies, media and financial intelligence units seems to foster self-reporting by companies, possibly because they may cause the company to fear detection through other information sources if it does not self-report.

3.4. Creating corporate liability systems

The key point made in the preceding section is that law enforcement authorities seeking to make efficient use of their resources should adopt policies to incentivize self-reporting as it is a reliable source of detection. Self-reporting and co-operation with law enforcement can be encouraged by building incentives into the law enforcement processes. But in order to do this, it has to be possible to hold companies liable for unlawful acts. Thus, the first and most basic incentive is to have laws in place that make companies liable for crimes committed in the context of their business operations.

Without corporate liability, only individuals are subject to criminal enforcement -- companies, as entities, cannot be the subject of law enforcement processes. As a result, law enforcement procedures are powerless to address the entire organisational dimension of economic crime.

This organisational dimension touches on many facets of activity within business organisations. For example, what incentives do employees face (e.g. are sales targets set so high that employees are implicitly encouraged to break the law in order to meet them)? What kinds of operational and financial information are collected and who has the authority to act on this information?

Under corporate liability laws, management processes themselves have a central role to play in enabling or preventing corporate crime; the responsibility of individuals, while extremely important, is seen as part of the larger picture of formal and informal practices within the company. Corporate liability systems allow law enforcement to incorporate this larger, managerial picture into their sanctioning processes.

At the end of the 20th century, many countries Party to the Anti-Bribery Convention did not have corporate liability but they agreed to create such systems when they acceded to the Convention, at least for foreign bribery (OECD, 1997, Article 2). OECD stocktaking shows that the countries Party to the Anti-Bribery Convention had very different starting points in this law-making process.[4] Sixteen of them had no established system for corporate liability prior to acceding to the Convention, except possibly in some areas of administrative law (e.g. tax and customs). For these countries, corporate liability was essentially a foreign concept, alien to their legal traditions and practices. They had to create their corporate liability systems 'from scratch'. In contrast, 25 countries had some prior legal basis for liability of legal persons, including codified law and judicial decisions.

Whether they were establishing systems for corporate liability for the first time or refining existing systems, all of the 41 Parties covered by the stocktaking exercise engaged in some kind of law-making activity relevant for corporate liability after the adoption of the Convention. Thus, after almost 20 years of intensive monitoring, all countries Party to the Anti-Bribery Convention can hold a corporation liable for the crime of foreign bribery[5] and many Parties are fine-tuning their systems. These systems are the starting point for creating a corporate role in corporate crime prevention and for motivating co-operation with law enforcement authorities in investigations and case resolutions.

3.5. Building incentives for compliance systems into the corporate liability system

"Compliance systems" are what managers put in place in order to reduce the risk that misconduct will occur in the context of their company's operations. Under some countries' corporate liability systems, the existence of a compliance system can completely preclude liability for foreign bribery. In such jurisdictions, it is up to the prosecutor to prove that the compliance system was not a genuine and well-designed effort to prevent crime.[6] In other countries, the company can use a compliance system to defend itself against charges – that is, if the company proves that its compliance system represented a serious attempt to deter criminal conduct, it cannot be held liable for unlawful conduct. For example, Australia provides that corporate liability will not apply "if the body corporate proves that it exercised due diligence to prevent the conduct".

Figure 3.3. Compliance systems as an element of the offence

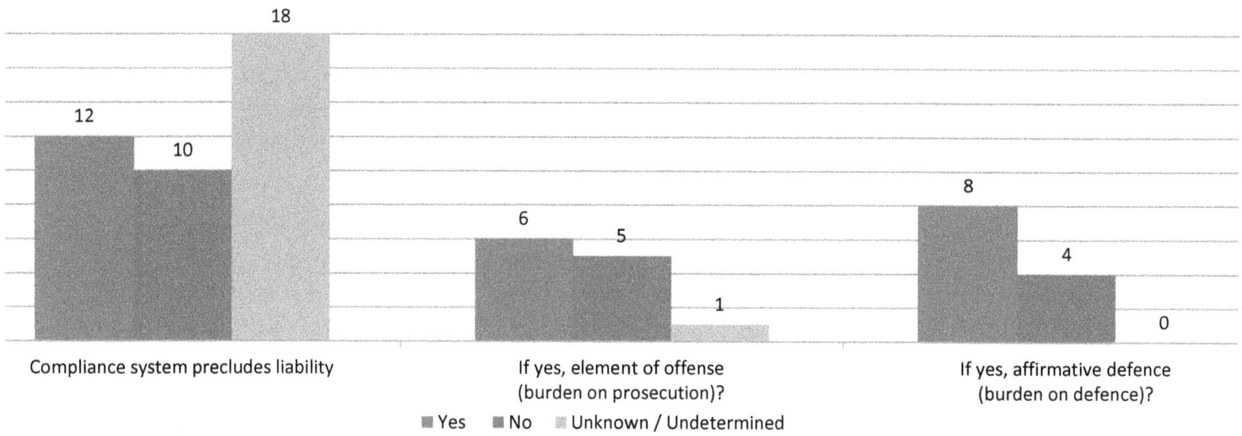

Source: OECD Working Group on Bribery's stocktaking exercise on liability of legal persons covering 41 Parties to the Anti-Bribery Convention.

Figure 3.4. Mitigating factors in company sanctions

(Number of resolution processes that permit consideration of different types of co-operation)

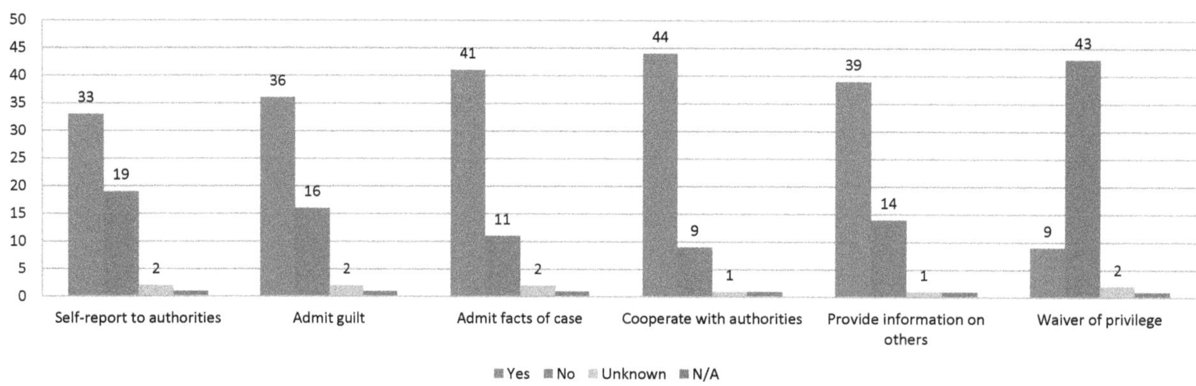

Source: OECD Working Group on Bribery's resolutions database.

Another approach (not mutually exclusive with the first) is to establish 'mitigating factors' that permit reductions in sanctions if the company self-reports and cooperates with law enforcement. Figure 3.4 shows how many Parties provide for reduction of sanctions in view of: (i) the existence and effectiveness of a compliance system, (ii) self-reporting suspicions of criminal activity to the authorities; and (iii) co-operation with investigations. These mitigating factors for sanctions are a key part of the incentive system that encourages companies to cooperate constructively with law enforcement authorities.

3.6. Building incentives for co-operation into the corporate liability system

Figure 3.5 shows that 14 Parties to the Convention allow for the reduction of corporate sanctions if the company cooperates with law enforcement authorities. Jurisdictions define in their own way what constitutes co-operation and concepts of co-operation vary across Parties. A broad definition of co-operation would mean that the company conducted timely and thorough internal investigations of suspected wrongdoing and disclosed the findings of these investigations to law enforcement authorities. Such disclosure would include providing to law enforcement authorities the information revealed by the internal investigation on culpable employees and business partners.[7]

As already noted, providing incentive for companies to cooperate (including through internal investigations) provides a number of benefits, both for themselves and for law enforcement. Companies can be more effective than outside law enforcement authorities at investigating suspected wrongdoing because they already know the details of their operating and financial activities. This then assists law enforcement authorities in making a thorough, timely and efficient investigation (including checking information provided by companies for accuracy and completeness). It also helps authorities to conduct investigations in ways that that minimise disruption to the company's legitimate business operations and that preserve procedural transparency and predictability.

Company investigations also have other procedural advantages. A company can conduct cross border investigations without facing the major procedural barriers that often confront law enforcement officials. Such legal barriers to international co-operation in law enforcement can include cumbersome procedures for obtaining legal assistance from foreign authorities (e.g. to seize evidence or to conduct interviews).[8] They may also constrain the uses to which such information may be put in a law enforcement context (e.g. evidence obtained from interviews conducted abroad might not be admissible in court). Finally, international investigations can be costly – creating incentives for companies to bear at least some of these costs allows for fuller internalisation of the costs of corporate crime since businesses then bear the cost of uncovering some of the facts associated with the wrongdoing.

The Siemens foreign bribery case provides insights into the details of internal investigations of company misconduct and shows how extensive these investigations can be. This case involved a global bribery scheme that straddled many of the markets in which Siemens did business. Bribery was deeply rooted in the company's corporate culture and affected company operations across the globe. In co-operation with a multi-jurisdictional law enforcement effort, Siemens conducted an internal investigation that is reported to have cost €550 million. According to settlement documents, Siemens hired more than 300 lawyers, forensic accountants and support staff from a law firm and an accounting firm for a two-year internal probe. The company estimated that the firms billed 1.5 million hours of legal and accountancy work. The investigation spanned 34 countries and included 1 750 interviews. Of the roughly 100 million documents collected in the investigation, Siemens produced about 24 000 documents for the US Department of Justice (Jones, 2012). Siemens settled with German and US law enforcement authorities in 2007 and 2008, respectively, and agreed to pay what were, at the time, record fines.

Figure 3.5. What types of co-operation are relevant for resolving cases with a legal person?

(Number of resolution processes that permit consideration of different types of co-operation)

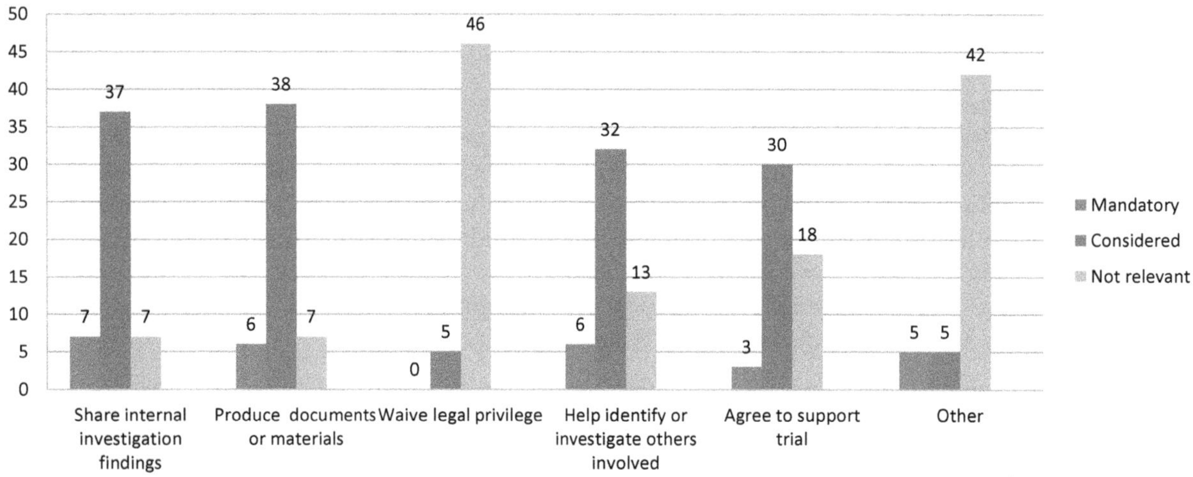

Source. OECD Working Group on Bribery's resolutions database.

3.7. Conclusions and additional considerations

Progress in creating legal frameworks. Legal systems change slowly, but over the 20 years since the Anti-Bribery Convention entered into force, Parties to the Convention have made significant progress in building the legal frameworks applying to unlawful conduct by corporations.

The creation and refinement of corporate liability systems are key elements of this progress. At the time the Anti-Bribery Convention entered into force, a third of the Parties had no legal framework for corporate liability and many of the others had only very sketchy systems that did not reflect the complexities of business management.[9] Now, all Parties to the Anti-Bribery Convention can hold business organisations liable for crime in some form or other. In most cases, corporate liability systems make companies accountable for foreign bribery and for a wide variety of other unlawful acts. This, along with the adoption of increasingly dissuasive sanctions for foreign bribery, strengthens incentives for companies to adopt management systems designed both to prevent corporate crime and to encourage them to cooperate with law enforcement.

As noted above, the current state of play in the area of corporate criminal law is one of great progress, but also of great variation in law and practice among Parties to the Anti-Bribery Convention.

- ***Strengthening newly established corporate liability systems***. Some countries are at the early stages of developing their corporate liability systems. They need to build on and refine their systems, including by adopting incentives for self-reporting and co-operation.

- ***Further improvements of long standing corporate liability systems in light of enforcement experience.*** Other countries have long traditions of corporate liability, but still need to fine-tune their systems. OECD monitoring shows that Parties to the Anti-Bribery Convention are refining their corporate liability systems in light of enforcement experience in order to obtain better outcomes. Some of the objectives of these refinements include:
  - Increasing public access to information about corporate resolutions. Making it possible for law enforcement authorities to release more information about the procedures and outcomes of the system (e.g. increasing public access to information about resolutions).
  - Clarifying and protecting the rights of individuals involved in cases concluded with corporate resolutions. As noted above, corporate investigations are not subject to the same procedural disciplines as investigations by law enforcement authorities. Although this has clear advantages in terms of rapidly generating relevant information, the law needs to ensure that the procedural rights of all parties to the investigation – including the individuals who may be implicated in the criminal activity -- are not infringed in the course of corporate co-operation with law enforcement authorities.
  - Managing how the systems interact internationally. The number of multi-jurisdictional corporate crime cases is increasing (OECD, 2017b). As a result, it has become increasingly apparent that the international enforcement community needs to refine the current *modus operandi* for co-operation in order to promote the orderly resolution of cases across jurisdictions. What are the rules for sharing information obtained from company self-reporting across jurisdictions? Does a resolution obtained by agreement between a company and law enforcement authorities in one country mean that that company cannot be held liable for the same offence in other countries? This work can be done on a country-by-country basis.

The creation of legal systems in general and of corporate liability in particular is an evolutionary process that involves continual adaptation and refinement. The OECD Working Group on Bribery provides a platform in which its members can share information and experiences and exert peer pressure in order to improve both their laws and their enforcement practices.

Notes

[1] Page 13 of OECD (2017a) states the following about self-reporting: 'Generally, the notion of self-reporting applies to companies, whereas individuals reporting themselves would be considered as confidential informants or cooperating witnesses. A company that self-reports will often also continue to provide ongoing co-operation with law enforcement authorities in the context of related investigation and related proceedings. There is currently no international anti-corruption standard relating specifically to self-reporting and practices vary across jurisdictions.'

[2] Enforcement experience in countries Party to the Anti-Bribery Convention has shown the significant degree to which lack of management systems and a tolerant corporate culture can lead to widespread criminal activity across through a company's business operations.

[3] This statistic reflects mainly the German tax authorities' role in detecting foreign bribery, which detected 17 cases, of which 11 resulted in at least one sanction on an individual or a corporate entity. Germany's Phase 4 Report notes the proactive role in detection of the German tax authorities (see, for example, page 5), www.oecd.org/corruption/anti-bribery/Germany-Phase-4-Report-ENG.pdf.

[4] As shown on page 8 of OECD (2016) and in Part 1 of this report, the development of corporate liability systems is an ongoing process, with virtually all countries Party to the Anti-Bribery Convention taking legislative action to establish and/ or refine their corporate liability systems.

[5] As shown on page 21 of OECD (2016), most countries Party to the Anti-Bribery Convention apply their corporate liability systems to a broader range of criminal activity than just foreign bribery and no Party to the Convention has a corporate liability system that applies only to foreign bribery.

[6] See page 66 of OECD (2016) for a discussion of where and under what circumstances compliances systems can preclude liability for foreign bribery.

[7] One public official participating in Working Group comment procedures noted that 'inviting companies to conduct investigations themselves could lead to unwarranted privilege claims. This can create satellite litigation and can take months or even years to resolve.'

[8] The EU's General Data Protection Regulation (GDPR) raises concerns for some countries in the area of cross border information sharing for law enforcement purposes. Countries are still exploring the impact that the GCPR will have on international co-operation in law enforcement.

[9] For example, many of the common law members of the Working Group on Bribery had a "directing mind" approach to the standard of corporate liability, meaning that involvement by the top decision-making echelons of the company must be proved, if liability is to be established.

References

Jones, M. (2012), 'The High Cost of Non-Compliance', *FCPA Compliance & Ethics,* http://fcpacompliancereport.com/2012/11/the-high-costs-of-non-compliance/.

OECD (2017a), *The Detection of Foreign Bribery,* www.oecd.org/corruption/the-detection-of-foreign-bribery.htm.

OECD (2017b), 2016 Data on Enforcement of the Anti-Bribery Convention: Special focus on international co-operation, www.oecd.org/daf/anti-bribery/Anti-Bribery-Convention-Enforcement-Data-2016.pdf.

OECD (2016), *The Liability of Legal Persons for Foreign Bribery: A Stocktaking Report,* www.oecd.org/corruption/liability-of-legal-persons-for-foreign-bribery-stocktaking-report.htm.

OECD (1997), OECD Convention on Combating Bribery of Foreign Public Officials in International Business Transactions, www.oecd.org/corruption/oecdantibriberyconvention.htm.

Chapter 4. Trust and the level playing field - The evolving state ownership

Chapter 4 applies a broad definition of "level playing field", which is taken to indicate different treatment of state-owned enterprises (SOEs) in the competitive landscape, with respect to corruption and other irregular practices, as well as the conduct of SOEs active in foreign jurisdictions. It demonstrates that SOEs active in certain sectors – notably steel production – tend to be less profitable than private peers, yet less likely to go out of business. Similarly, SOEs appear to have a heightened risk of getting involved in some forms of corruption, but they are less likely than private companies to divest from certain projects or disengage from business partners due to integrity concerns. The chapter finally takes stock of ongoing OECD initiatives that either aim directly at, or could have as an outcome, raising trust in state-owned enterprises and their commercial operations.

The increasing presence of state-owned enterprises (SOEs) in the global economy has given rise to concerns about preserving a level playing field between companies owned by sovereign states and the rest of the business sector. One rationale for state ownership of enterprises is that market failures lead the state to create SOEs and obliges them to help meet public policy objectives. While in some cases the state accurately calculates the cost of meeting those objectives, and provides appropriate reimbursement, in others the SOE is over-compensated, for instance through preferential treatment. Support might be justified as long as these benefits accurately match the costs incurred by the companies in carrying out their public policy obligation – but in practice this can become highly complex when the SOEs pursue a variety of objectives that might lead to internal conflicts or trade-offs. The challenge for both regulators and the state acting as an enterprise owner is to build trust that SOEs will operate according to generally accepted corporate practices when active in competitive markets. Among the areas of current concern to OECD governments are:

- *Competitive neutrality.* One of the most pertinent sources of unease about SOEs is the fear among their competitors that they enjoy undue state support that may take a number of forms including direct market-distorting subsidies, preferential market access, regulatory forbearance and unreasonably low rates of return on the capital invested. This, in turn, could either allow artificially profitable SOEs to crowd out more productive competitors, or allow financially weaker SOEs to stay in markets where a comparable private operator would have ceased operations.
- *SOE integrity.* Another trust issue arises from a widely held perception that SOEs are prone to get involved in corruption scandals and other irregular practices. State ownership matters in this context because, first, enterprises operating closely to the public authorities might perceive a degree of impunity. Secondly, if SOEs are insufficiently separated from the functions of the state they can become embroiled in more widespread irregularities within national political systems. Where this is the case the playing field is uneven since SOEs then effectively operate subject to different rules.
- *Cross-border operations.* When state-owned enterprises operate abroad, they are sometimes viewed with scepticism in their host country. In some cases they may be mistrusted because certain of the objectives of state ownership are either ill understood or perceived as illegitimate. In other cases there may be a perception that they benefit from a privileged position in their home jurisdictions which can confer competitive advantages abroad. In addition to such competitive-neutrality related issues, some SOE objectives may be perceived as posing threats to host countries' essential security interests. This brings at risk both the national competitive landscape and the level playing field among nations.

4.1. The global SOE landscape

Evidence of the growing importance of SOEs in the global economy is most visible at the top of the "corporate league table" since in almost all economies SOEs are on average larger than private firms. Currently, 102 of the world's largest 500 enterprises (measured by annual revenues) are wholly or majority owned by sovereign governments. The trend is upward. Less than two decades ago 34 of the largest enterprises were state-owned – in other words, the state's share has trebled (Figure 4.1).

The significant shift is mostly because of the growing prominence of China's SOEs. In 2000, there were eight Chinese firms among the top-500, whereas today's number stands at 74.[1] The importance of SOEs in other emerging markets has also grown, with the number of large SOEs in India, Brazil and Russia growing and a number of new countries seeing their national SOEs appear on the list (e.g. Mexico, Indonesia, Saudi Arabia and Thailand). Conversely, the prevalence and size of SOEs in European countries as well as Japan have waned during the period under review. The geographic shift from OECD countries toward emerging economies has been accompanied by sectoral change, since SOEs in advanced economies are mostly found in the network industries and hydrocarbons sectors (plus in some cases finance), while in emerging countries they can be found among a much broader range of economic activities.

Figure 4.1. SOEs among the world's largest 500 enterprises

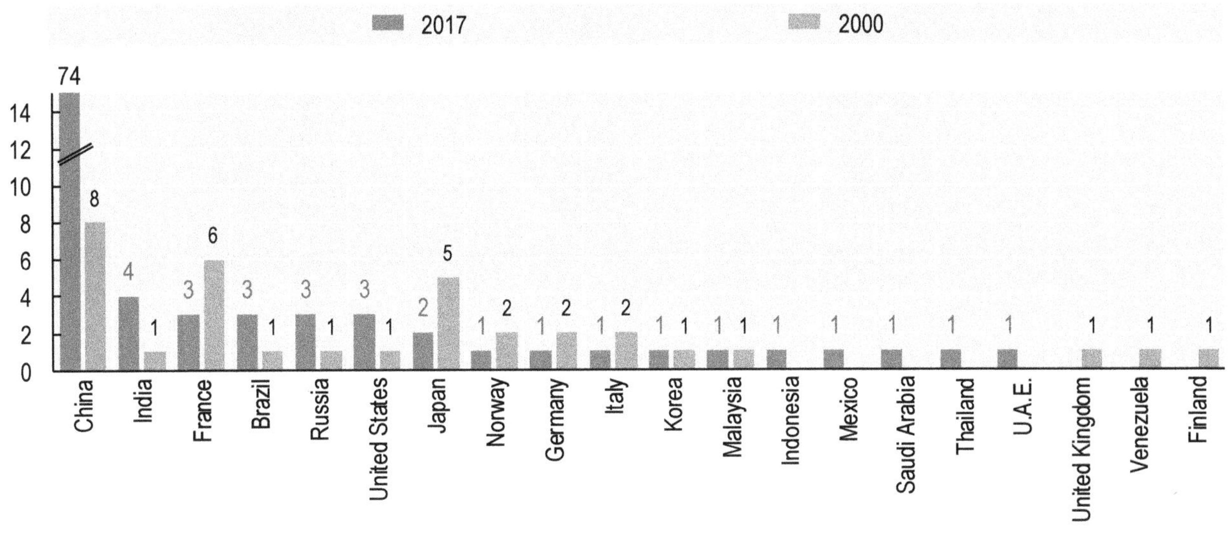

Source: OECD calculations based on Fortune Global 500.

4.1.1. A granular look: SOEs in the infrastructure sector

In countries that have had active privatisation programmes in the past, many or most of the remaining SOEs tend to be found in the infrastructure sectors. Mostly this reflects the fact that they have either monopoly positions in certain market segments or are subject to an array of public policy objectives that would make them hard to privatise. Figure 4.2 illustrates the relative importance of this sector in the SOE portfolios of OECD member governments. This in turn implies that a successful implementation of the policies seen in some countries of supporting national recovery via infrastructure spending, as well as a pent-up need for investment in some others, will depend strongly on well-functioning SOEs.

New approaches to infrastructure investment are also being developed, including through public-private partnerships (PPPs). Recent data shows that more than USD 93 billion worth of PPPs in the infrastructure sector were contracted in 2018.[2] Through PPPs important economic gains can be made, if for example the state's access to low-interest financing is combined with the higher operational efficiency of private sector operators. Conversely, relying solely on private sector finance is often not an optimal solution and can in some cases be little more than an attempt to shift debt off the public sector balance sheet.

Figure 4.2. State-owned enterprises in the infrastructure sector

Percentage share of OECD total SOE portfolio

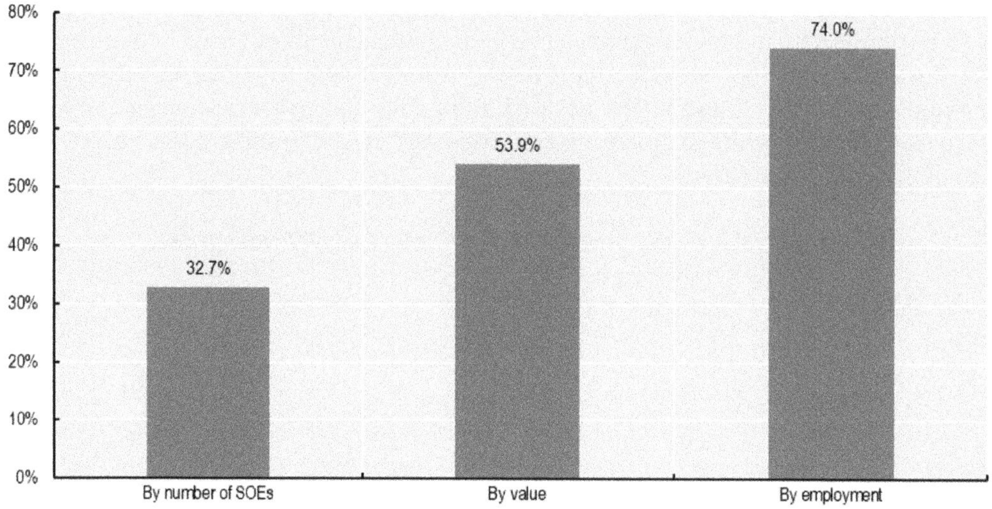

Note: The figure is based on a definition which includes in the infrastructure sector "transportation", "energy" and "other utilities". Notably, this excludes telecommunication.
Source: OECD (2017).

PPPs may involve SOEs in several ways. First, the state often participates in the partnership via an existent state-owned enterprise, or establishes a new operation company to oversee the PPP. Secondly, a surprisingly high proportion of the "private" participants tend to be state controlled – and typically operating outside their domestic jurisdictions. More than 19% of the infrastructure PPPs launched in 2018 involved public institutions, roughly half of which SOEs and the other half state-controlled institutional investors.

4.1.2. State ownership of stock-market listed companies

Governments have also become important shareholder owners in many stock markets, mainly as a result of partial privatisations through stock market listings. In many cases, divestment through the stock market has not led to any change in control, as governments remained as largest shareholder in the newly listed companies. Figure 4.3 illustrates the level of government ownership of stock market listed companies. In Lithuania, Saudi Arabia; Hong Kong, China and Malaysia, for example, governments hold on average over 40% of the capital. In the case of Hong Kong, China, the large non-domestic government ownership represents the Chinese government ownership. In 15 out of the 53 markets shown in the figure, governments hold more than 20% of the capital of listed corporations.

In the context of trust in a level playing field, key questions relate to SOE performance and financial structures relative to private competitors. Table 4.1 summarises performance and leverage indicators for SOEs and non-SOEs in each market. SOEs are defined broadly to include those where government are the ultimate beneficiary owners of at least 20% of the capital. In most of the economies under review SOEs display significantly poorer rates of return than private firms. At the same time SOEs exhibit higher leverage in most markets compared to non-SOEs companies.[3] This could indicate a higher degree of risk willingness on the part of these companies as well as their creditors, which in this case may well be linked to their proximity to the state.

Figure 4.3. Government ownership of listed companies, end 2017

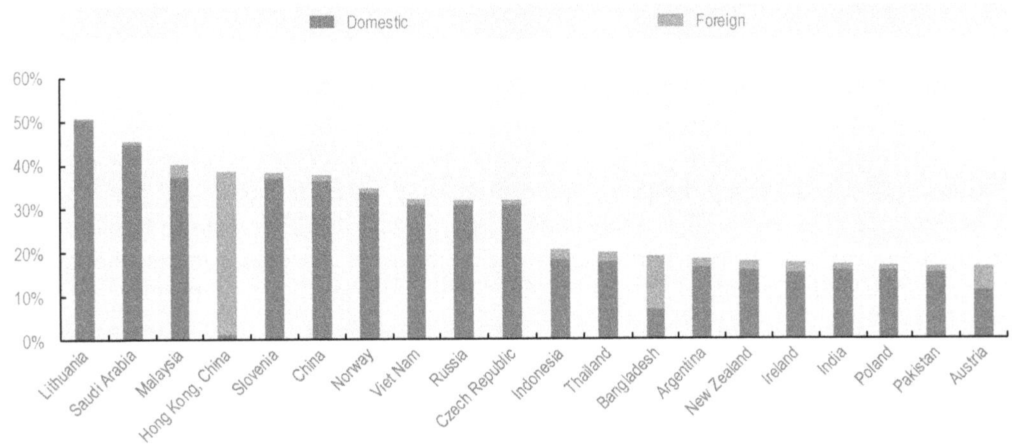

Note: The table shows market capitalisation weighted average ownership for governments. Calculations are based on ownership data for at least 80% of market capitalisation in each jurisdiction. The countries included in the table are the ones in the sample where the SOE segment of the stock market is at least one fifth of the total number of listed companies.
Source: OECD Capital Market Series dataset, FactSet.

Table 4.1. Performance and leverage for SOEs and non-SOEs, end 2017

	Number of companies		Average leverage			Average performance		
	SOEs	Non-SOEs	SOEs	Non-SOEs	Difference	SOEs	Non-SOEs	Difference
China	470	823	41.5%	15.5%	26%	6.7%	10.8%	-4%
Hong Kong, China	98	132	69.7%	45.9%	24%	8.8%	14.8%	-6%
Hungary	3	7	21.3%	33.4%	-12%	7.4%	9.2%	-2%
Indonesia	15	47	58.3%	54.6%	4%	10.3%	21.3%	-11%
Lithuania	3	11	29.2%	22.1%	7%	3.7%	12.0%	-8%
Malaysia	44	61	63.7%	30.8%	33%	20.4%	19.0%	1%
Russia	31	45	50.6%	88.7%	-38%	5.0%	55.0%	-50%
Saudi Arabia	21	45	67.8%	36.4%	31%	14.7%	15.8%	-1%
Slovenia	6	3	49.3%	62.7%	-13%	6.9%	-1.5%	8%
Viet Nam	19	37	33.4%	39.3%	-6%	22.9%	18.0%	5%

Note: The table excludes financial companies. State owned enterprises (SOEs) are identified as companies where governments own at least 20% of the capital. Non-SOEs are identified as companies with less than 20% government ownership. Leverage is computed as the 5-year average of $\frac{long\text{-}term\ debt_t}{total\ capital_t}$ and performance as the 5-year average of $\frac{net\ income_t}{total\ capital_{t-1}}$. The columns "difference" report the average leverage (performance) in SOEs minus average leverage (performance) in non-SOEs. The markets in the in the figure have at least 20% of its companies defined as an SOE.
Source: OECD Capital Market Series dataset, FactSet.

These finding lend themselves to the interpretation that there may be little evidence that SOEs in general, insofar as they enjoy benefits from their ownership, translate this into either high performance or a cushioned balance sheet. Rather, they could be underperforming in both respects and avoid having to take corrective action or exit the market due to a continued support from the state. An alternative interpretation might be that SOEs tend to be concentrated in areas and sectors that are often avoided by private investors on account of low profitability.

4.2. State-owned enterprises and the maintenance of a vibrant competition landscape

This section sheds light on two important trust-related aspects of SOEs' conduct in competitive markets. First, is there a risk that they could benefit from their ownership to crowd out more efficient competitors? If this is the case it can take a multitude of forms, including outright market-distorting subsidies, artificially low rates of return or a privileged position in their domestic markets. An illustrative case arises from the steel and shipbuilding sectors where it is frequently alleged that SOEs contribute to a persistent overcapacity in international markets. Secondly, SOEs actions in competitive markets, including their commitment to a level playing field and compliance with competition law more generally, is an area of interest. State-owned enterprises are overseen by politicians and/or high-level government officials and are widely perceived as setting the "tone at the top" in national corporate landscapes. Examples of unhealthy competitive practices by SOEs are liable to lead to a loss of public trust in the state as well as in the business sector.

4.2.1. The presence and financial performance of SOEs in the shipbuilding and steel industries

The widespread presence of the state in the shipbuilding and steel markets has raised concerns related to the beneficial treatment that state-owned enterprises possibly receive from their governments, the market-distortions that such treatment can generate, and the implications for excess capacity in these sectors. While definitions of SOEs vary and might not cover the full extent of state control, available indicators for shipbuilding and steel suggest a significant presence of the state in these two sectors.

Figure 4.4. Ship completions by state-owned and other firms, 2008-2017

Completion in GT (top 20 shipyards)

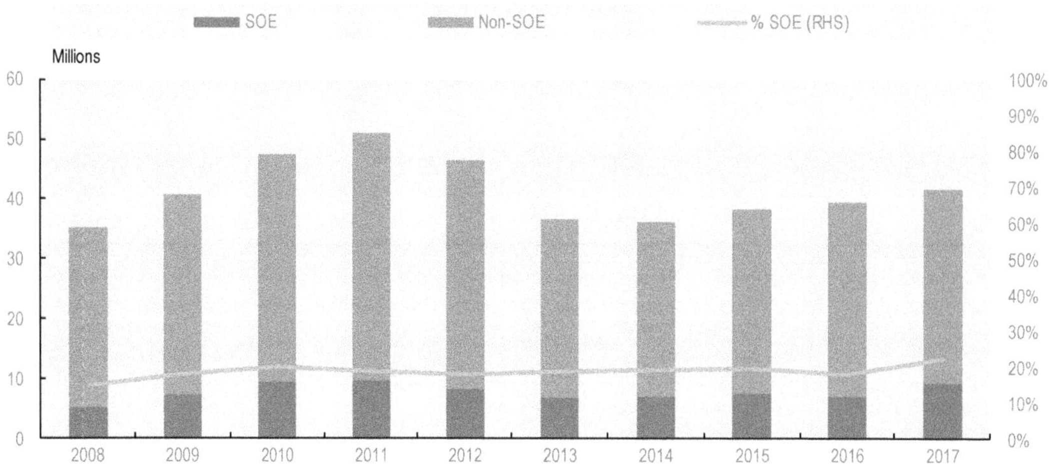

Source: OECD calculations based on Clarkson World Fleet Register database.

The studied sample comprises the world's 20 largest yards, and it follows the definitions of the Clarkson World Fleet Register database concerning whether a given company is considered as an SOE. The data show that SOEs play a large role in the global shipbuilding industry, with seven SOEs among the top 20 companies by completion in gross tonnage (GT) terms. These seven SOEs, all of which are located in China, represent 22% of total ship completions of the top 20 companies. The share of SOEs in ship completions has fluctuated slightly, from 15% to 22% over the last decade (Figure 4.4).

The steel industry is more geographically diverse than shipbuilding, with hundreds of companies in around 100 economies involved in crude steel production. Similar to shipbuilding, the state accounts for a large share of the sector's output. In 2016, state enterprises produced at least 522 mmt of crude steel in 2016, accounting for at least 32% of global crude steel production that year.[4] In addition, 22 of the world's largest 100 crude steel-producing companies were either directly or indirectly linked to some degree of state ownership. Steel production by state enterprises takes place entirely in non-OECD economies, particularly in East and South Asia as well as in the Middle East.

Figure 4.5. Steel production by state-owned enterprises and other firms, 2016

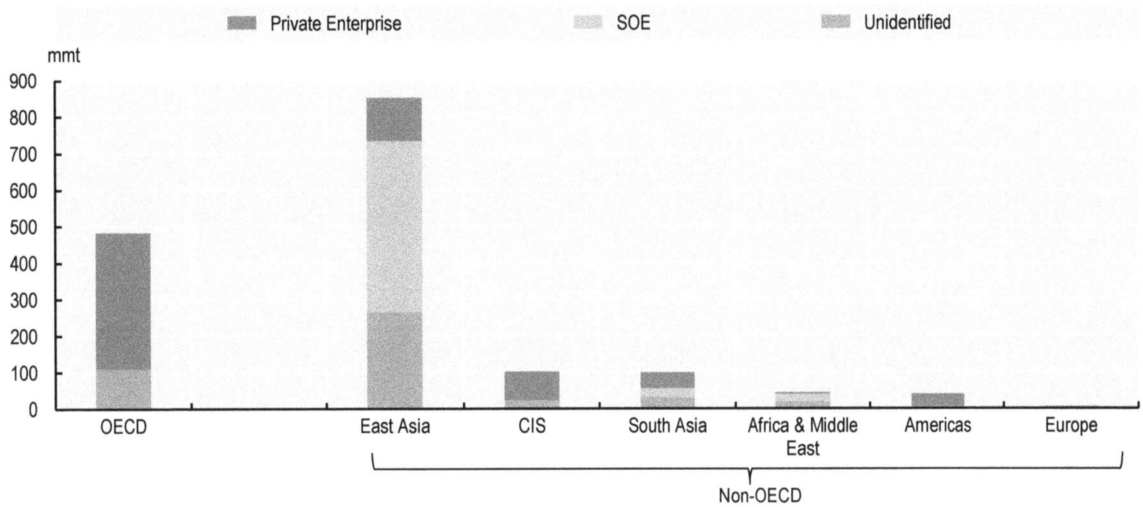

Note: The chart represents 2016 steel production figures (mmt) at regional level by ownership type. The column on the left group together the total crude steel production for all OECD/EU economies. Columns on the right side include production data for all non-OECD/EU economies by region. Figures for SOEs and Private Enterprises refer to crude steelmaking production for the top 100 steelmaking companies. "Unidentified" stands for all the remaining crude steel produced by companies that are not in the list of the 100 largest steelmakers.
Source: OECD calculations based on data from the World Steel Association and ORBIS (OECD (2018c).

Are state owned steel firms less profitable than their private counterparts?

Firm-level data containing information on ownership and financial indicators shows that state enterprises in the steel sector are characterised by a lower level of profitability (Figure 4.6). This is backed-up by recent work within the OECD Steel Committee which shows that, after controlling for a number of aspects that can influence firms' financial performance, there is a negative and statistically significant relationship between state ownership status and profit margins, suggesting that state enterprises are less efficient than private entities at least when it comes to steel (OECD, 2018c). Such inefficiencies in steel state enterprises may arise from governance, suboptimal incentives to public management and/or relaxed budget constraints associated with public support or lax regulation.

While there may be rationales for state ownership, concerns have been raised regarding the potential lack of transparency and preferential treatment granted to SOEs. This may result in distortions and contribute to excess capacity in some sectors. In the steel sector, recent research shows that most of the plant closures in recent years have affected private companies, despite their higher average profitability (see Table 4.2). Data on recent investments in steelmaking capacity around the globe also suggest that a considerable share of planned and on-going capacity investments are being implemented (Table 4.3). Here the picture is more mixed: both SOEs and private enterprises plan or are currently implementing, such investments. The data do, however, suggest that going forward the balance between capacity in OECD and non-OECD countries is likely to tip further toward the latter.

Figure 4.6. Profit margins by ownership type

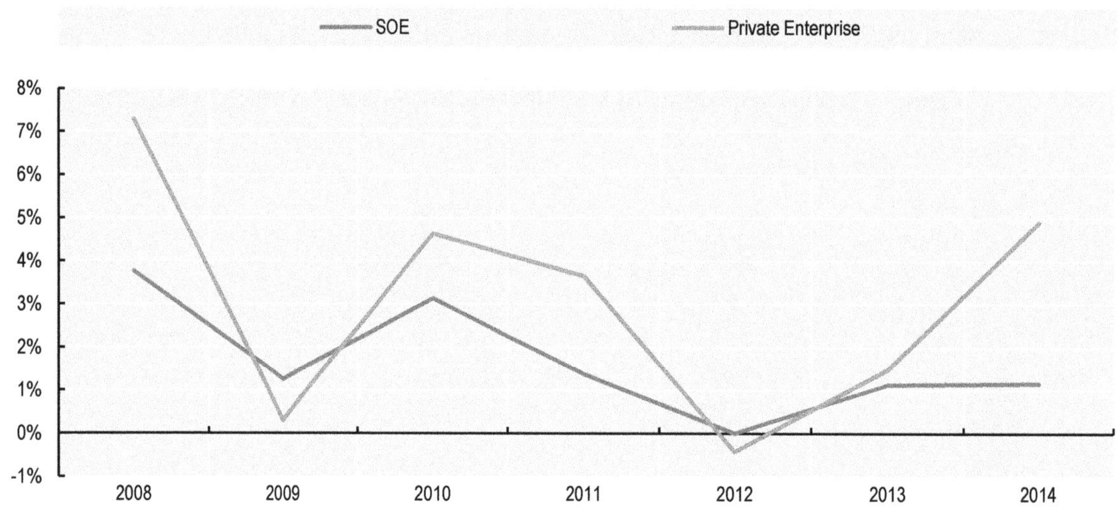

Note: The chart compares the average net profits of all SOEs companies, with the average net profits of an equivalent number of private enterprises with the same characteristics.
Source: OECD calculations based on data from ORBIS.

Table 4.2. Capacity closures by ownership type

Data covers 2016 and 2017

	Number of closures		Capacity closed (mmt)	
	SOEs	Private Enterprises	SOEs	Private Enterprises
OECD	0	11	0	13.4
non-OECD	14	16	7.6	8.7

Source: OECD (2018c).

Table 4.3. Investments in new steel capacity by ownership type

Crude steelmaking capacity investment projects (expected to be) deployed between 2012 and 2025

	Operating/Underway			Planned		
Capacity (mmt)	*SOEs*	*Private Enterprises*	*Unidentified*	*SOEs*	*Private Enterprises*	*Unidentified*
OECD	0	25.8	1.9	0	24.9	11.1
non-OECD	152.7	120.3	46.2	97.4	133.2	22.1
No. investments	*SOEs*	*Private Enterprises*	*Unidentified*	*SOEs*	*Private Enterprises*	*Unidentified*
OECD	0	15	4	0	9	9
non-OECD	70	89	52	41	50	34

Source: OECD (2018c).

4.3. State ownership and competition regulation

4.3.1. Competitive neutrality

The issues that have arisen in steel markets are just one example of the types of competitive distortion that can result from misguided intervention by governments. To guard against these risks, governments can establish rules for competitive neutrality in order to help build trust in a level playing field – i.e. ensuring that no enterprises are advantaged, or disadvantaged in a way that prevents, restricts or distorts competition within a market. Such rules consider the competitive effect of actions by government that create an advantage or disadvantage based on an enterprises' ownership and legal status, as well as the location of their activities or head office, their public service obligations, their importance as a major employer, their proximity to the state power, their systemic importance, their market dominance, or their charitable status. A related distortion of the competition landscape may occur where SOEs – typically within the financial sector – are used by their government owners to grant subsidies and other concessionary treatment to private companies (or other SOEs) active in competitive markets.

Where markets are distorted by such factors, consumers may find it worthwhile to purchase from less efficient firms, and even where efficient firms did manage to survive and thrive, they might face less competitive pressure and thus set higher prices or innovate less. Furthermore competitors in the market might not be able to trust that their comparative advantage will not be artificially diminished, thereby reducing their incentive to invest.

Prominent examples of countries with rules on these matters include a comprehensive competitive neutrality framework in Australia, the implementation of which is overseen by an autonomous body, the Productivity Commission. Specific rules on anticompetitive conduct by SOEs are moreover in place in Sweden and other Nordic countries. In some countries, competitive neutrality principles are enshrined in the constitution (e.g. Brazil, Chile, Mexico and the Russian Federation). In most jurisdictions, competition authorities have "soft" powers allowing them to recommend changes in regulatory framework or in legal provisions, which may lead to a distortion of competitive neutrality. China recently saw an introduction of such rules in its Fair Competition Review System.

Concerns have however been voiced as to whether purely domestic rules are sufficient and adequate. This question has come up for instance when companies domiciled in strictly rules-based domestic environments face international competition from firms that are not subject to similar constraints. This might justify an international approach to rule making. Indeed, rules on competitive neutrality do already exist at an international level, for example the European Union has wide-ranging state aid rules as well as public procurement directives.

The WTO also has rules on subsidies and a general procurement agreement. Though complaints and enforcement under WTO rules operate at a governmental level and are not open to enterprises themselves. Enforcement and complaints under EU State aid rules are not limited to the governmental level. Given the possible impact of state aid on competition, enterprises play an important role. They can lodge complaints with the European Commission against state aids granted by an EU Member State, and can also intervene during formal investigation procedures on state aid cases. If a State is found to have granted unlawful state aid, the benefitting enterprise has to pay it back, which resolves the distortion by removing the aid, rather than allowing other States to match it, and thereby prevents expensive subsidy battles. An overview of tools and mechanisms for maintaining a level playing field in some economies is provided in Table 4.4.

Table 4.4. Examples of measures to ensure a level playing field amid state ownership and controls

Distortion	Tools	Jurisdiction	Relevant Authority
State- controlled market player	Corporate governance	Italy	Competition Authority
	Transparency rules (legislation & guidelines)	European Union	n.a
	Rationalise the number of SOEs	Chinese Taipei	Task Force for Facilitating Privatization of Public Enterprises
	Tax neutrality, Rate of return policy for public undertakings	Spain	Ministry of Economic and Finance
	Debt neutrality	Australia	Australian Government
Public service obligations	Open, fair and transparent bidding process	Australia	Australian Government
	Accounting separation rules	European Union	European Commission
	Reimbursement for public service obligation rules	European Union	European Commission
	Structural separation	Sweden	Competition Authority
	Access equality	The Netherlands	Competition Authority
	Benchmark for compensation, accounting for public service obligation	Hungary	State Aid Monitoring Office
Subsidies	Ex ante and ex-post state aid control (including the possibility to order the benefitting enterprise to reimburse unlawful state aid)	European Union	European Commission
	Mechanism to supervise the use of public funds	Spain	General State Controller, Regional Controllers
Sectoral regulation	Regulatory impact assessment	Finland	Competition Authority
	Market studies and advocacy	United Kingdom	Competition Authority
	Ex ante policy co-ordination	Japan	Competition Authority
	Disapply or denouncing the regulation	Peru	Competition Authority
	Judicial review	Italy	Competition Authority

Source: Authors' compilation, based on OECD (2015b).

The perhaps most frequently aired complaint about an uneven playing field relates to SOEs' supposedly easier access to finance. At issue is SOEs access to credits from state-controlled financial institution, as well as more broadly the fact that private banks are often willing to make funds available at preferential rates due to actual or perceived state guarantees for SOE debt. This could be linked to a broader corporate issue, as SOEs tend to be significantly larger than private firms. Small and medium-sized enterprises (SMEs) are often thought to be at a competitive disadvantage in their access to bank credits which, insofar as this reflects discrimination rather than a higher default risk among the SMEs, adds an important additional dimension to concerns about a level playing field.

4.3.2. Anti-trust enforcement in the presence of SOEs

Rigorous antitrust enforcement, applied regardless of ownership, nationality, legal or financing status, plays a key role in levelling the playing field. For instance it directly addresses those cases where a dominant firm, whether it be a privately owned enterprise, or a domestic or foreign state owned enterprise is able to distort competition to exclude rivals. However, investigations against SOEs can pose a variety of challenges due to the distinctive nature of SOEs, and additional difficulties can emerge when foreign SOEs are involved.

An initial challenge is that, as most competition standards are based on enterprises having profit maximising objectives and facing a level playing field, neutral enforcement might require adapting the analytical tools typically applied in competition proceedings to reflect the advantages that SOEs may benefit from. For example, in the case of predatory pricing strategies, SOEs' characteristics and privileged position can affect their costs, and thus the use of recoupment tests and cost-benchmarks for enforcers.

In the assessment of specific anti-competitive behaviours, another challenge can arise when defining the SOE's economic entity in mergers and antitrust cases, as the extent of the State's involvement in the SOE's decision-making process is not always clear-cut. This aspect will also influence the calculation of turnover, central to establish the need for notification of a merger or the appropriate fine in a cartel case. These considerations are particularly relevant when SOEs are involved in cross-border cases, as governance systems might vary and their functioning may be difficult to grasp correctly.

Different accounting standards for SOEs and lack of transparency regarding costs can also make it burdensome for agencies to obtain relevant information from SOEs, on which to base their assessment. Moreover, effective enforcement against anticompetitive conduct by SOEs also requires effective sanctions for such entities. However, fines may be less effective deterrents to anticompetitive conduct by SOEs that can pass them onto taxpayers. Finally, SOEs might also have means to obstruct proceedings if their government ties play a role, e.g. in the form of possible explicit or implicit government pressure during an investigation against an SOE. It is therefore important to maintain the independence of competition authorities.[5] Table 4.5 provides examples of a number of cases where the relevant competition authority had to address issues linked to the involvement of one or more SOEs, domestic or foreign, in the investigation.

Table 4.5. Recent competition enforcement involving SOEs

Issue	Case	Type	Conduct	Jurisdiction
Definition of the economic entity	China Ocean Shipping Tally Shenzhen/China United Tally (Shenzhen)[1]	Domestic	Cartel	People's Republic of China
	EDF/CGN/NNB Group of Companies[2]	Foreign	Merger	European Union
Involvement of foreign SOEs: definition of the economic entity and weight of a foreign state's interpretation of its own legislation	Vitamin C: Animal Science Products, Inc. v. Hebei Welcome Pharmaceutical Co., 585 U.S.	Foreign	Cartel	United States
Involvement of foreign SOEs: access to information	Gazprom[3]	Foreign	Abuse of dominance	European Union
Involvement of foreign SOEs: application of the act of state doctrine	ESSA/Mitsubishi[4]	Foreign	Exclusive distribution agreements	United States
Cost-benchmarks used in predatory pricing	Deutsche Post AG[5]	Domestic	Predatory pricing	European Union
Effectiveness of sanctions	South African Airlines (multiple cases)[6]	Domestic	Abuse of dominance and cartel behaviour	South Africa

1. Decision at http://samr.saic.gov.cn/gg/201807/t20180720_275163.html (Chinese only).
2. Case No. COMP/M.7850.
3. Commission decision of 24.05.2018, Case AT.39816 – Upstream gas supplies in Central and Eastern Europe.
4. Sea Breeze Salt, Inc. et al. v. Mitsubishi Corp. et al., CV 16-2345-DMG, ECF No. 45 (Aug. 18, 2016) and Sea Breeze Salt, Inc. v. Mitsubishi Corp., No. 16-56350 (9th Cir. 2018).
5. Case COMP/35.141.
6. See South Africa contribution paper to OECD 2018 Roundtable on Competition Law And State-Owned Enterprises.
Source: Authors' compilation.

As neutral enforcement of merger control and antitrust rules has an important role in helping achieve competitive neutrality, factors that can create challenges for competition authorities and potentially lead to under or over-enforcement need to be constantly taken into account and assessed on a case-by-case basis. This will help to send a signal to all enterprises that anti-competitive conduct will be prosecuted, thus building trust in the existence of a level playing field.

4.4. The risk of corruption and irregular practices in the state-owned sector

State-owned enterprises have figured prominently in corruption-related prosecutions in recent years. The majority of bribe payments aimed at foreign public officials that were detected between 1999 and 2014 were destined for SOE employees and managers (OECD, 2014).[6] A recent OECD survey of board members and senior management in hundreds of large, economically significant SOEs showed that almost half of the companies (and 42% of the individuals) had witnessed corrupt acts or related irregular practices within their organisations in recent years (OECD, 2018a).

Citizens, as the ultimate shareholder, should be able to trust that SOEs and the state owner limit the potential for the abuse of SOEs or by SOEs for private gain. In turn, an active and professional state owner should expect that SOEs are behaving in line with state requirements and laws, including those relating to integrity and anti-corruption. SOEs should expect that state representatives will not seek to unduly influence the company's operations. Failing at any one of these outcomes can mean a simultaneous loss of the public's trust in SOEs and the state. The achievement of such outcomes – mitigating the omnipresent risk of corruption and embedding integrity in the SOE sector – is ultimately a job for both SOEs and their state owners.

4.4.1. What are the reputational and economic fallouts of SOE corruption?

The benefits of SOE ownership are economic, political and social – and so too are the costs of SOE corruption and irregular practices. The costs borne by SOEs or the state (and even society) can come in the form of sanctions, diversion of funds to illicit purposes or in foregone productivity gains of unfair market competition among others. Corruption or exploitation of SOEs can impact the delivery of critical public services. It can be damaging for political officials or entities responsible for SOE oversight and detrimental to the public's faith in democratic processes and institutions. Recent corruption-related scandals have shown how quickly trust in SOEs and the state as owner can be damaged.

Recent examples include two SOEs that were the targets of two of the largest FCPA enforcement actions of all time. The "Operação Lava Jato" ("Operation Car Wash"), putting Brazil's state-owned oil company, Petrobras, at the centre of an extensive trans-national bribery scheme involving multiple Brazilian construction conglomerates. Operation Car Wash had a chilling effect on the perceptions of society regarding politicians and political processes. With convictions of political figures, the scandal has reinforced the perception among many that the government is not acting in the public interest but for private interests (OECD, 2018b).

In another highly publicised case the SOE, somewhat more unusually, appeared as the bribe payer. In 2017, Swedish state-owned telecommunications company Telia was handed the largest global settlement of the time, amounting to USD 965 million, for violating the FCPA and making corrupt payments related to its market entry into Uzbekistan in 2007. Telia suffered not only financial losses. After receipt of the 2017 settlement, Telia's

President and Chief Executive referred to the company's efforts, following management and leadership changes in 2013, to "regain trust from all [our] stakeholders", citing it as "a never-ending journey as we aspire to embed this into our culture making sure that all employees understand the importance of doing the right thing all the time" (Telia, 2017).

4.4.2. What are the main risks of corruption and other rule-breaking in SOEs?

SOEs face corruption-related risks that are both external and internal to the company. As mentioned, almost half of the surveyed SOEs reported that such risks materialised in their company in the last three years. Such occurrences resulted more likely from the override of or ignorance to controls, rather than their absence. Indeed, SOEs reported that their main obstacles to improving integrity in their company as (i) a lack of a culture of integrity in the political and public sector; (ii) a lack of awareness among employees of the need for, or priority placed on, integrity, and (iii) opportunistic behaviour of individuals.

When it comes to the likelihood of rule-breaking there are important sectoral differences between SOEs. The 2018 report showed that SOEs in the oil and gas sector are particularly likely to have experienced corruption and other irregularities, followed by mining and the utilities sectors (Figure 4.7). A straightforward interpretation is that the incentives and opportunity for corruption are greater in SOEs that handle large financial flows, whether in the form of concessions or large-scale public procurement projects.

Figure 4.7. Those who reported witnessing corruption and other irregular practices, by sector of respondent

Sectors of respondents that said "yes" to "in your assessment, did any of the [listed] risks materialise into activities/actions in the last three years in (or involving) your company?"

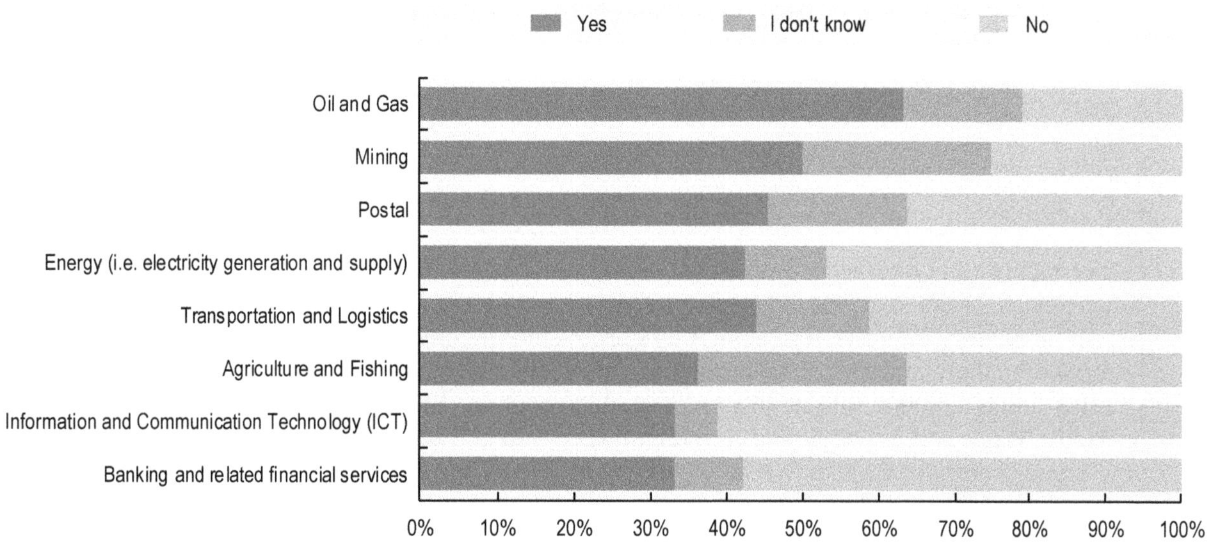

Note: Based on 289 responses falling into the retained 8 categories with more than 10 respondents.
Source: OECD (2018b).

Not all types of rule-breaking are equally likely to materialise, or equally damaging if they do materialise, and may depend on sector and country of operation. OECD (2018b) provides a heat-risk mapping of corruption-related risks of the surveyed SOEs for their likelihood of occurrence and theoretical impact. The aggregated survey data showed that receiving bribes is considered more likely than offering bribes. This is consistent with the aforementioned Foreign Bribery Report findings. SOEs are also concerned about risks that, while not explicitly corruption, may be representative of control weaknesses or vulnerabilities of the company.

SOEs' exposure to corruption may be influenced by SOEs ownership or market position, often in high-value sectors with frequent transactions. Opportunistic actors may feel protected by a perception that SOEs may be insulated by state ownership, or seek to exploit an SOEs' market-dominant position or involvement in the delivery of public services. Moreover, SOEs are protected from a threat of bankruptcy or hostile take-over that private companies face. Risks of corruption in SOEs may or may not be qualitatively different from private firms, but the OECD survey found that SOEs in some cases appear less able or less willing than private firms to avoid known high-risk activities.[7] Table 4.6 shows that private firms were approximately twice as likely as SOEs to take decisions that mitigate known risks of corruption.

Table 4.6. Actions taken by SOEs in the face of corruption risks

Action	SOEs	Non SOEs
Respondents said their companies have ceased business operations in a particular jurisdiction because of the integrity or corruption risks involved	12%	39%
Respondents that said their companies have taken internal remedial/disciplinary action following violation of your organisation's integrity or anti-corruption policies.	46%	70%
Respondents said their companies have substantially revised at least one business project because of the corruption and integrity risk(s) involved.	30%	66%
Respondents that said their companies severed a relationship with at least one business partner (e.g. supplier, service provider) because of the risk of exposure to or engaging in corruption.	32%	66%

Note: This analysis is done on 261 individual responses – not by company. Broad comparisons made with a survey of non-SOEs where the number of respondents was 57.
Source: OECD (2018b).

4.5. Concerns about threats to essential security interests resulting from SOEs' operations abroad

Governments that own enterprises most often pursue specific policy objectives with these enterprises. These may include non-commercial objectives such as safeguarding their essential security interests, for instance by keeping closer control over critical infrastructure operated by these enterprises; or ensuring availability and supply under volatile or adverse market conditions that private owned companies may not be able to withstand for longer periods. Many of these objectives are legitimate when and where they are associated with the home country of a given SOE.

When SOEs are allowed or encouraged to operate abroad, host countries of their investments may perceive some of these non-commercial objectives in a different light: the intentions and objectives of the home country may conflict with the essential security interests of the host country of SOEs' investments. Also, the host country may suspect that the foreign SOE may threaten its essential security interest directly. It could perceive the SOE as a front used by the home government for espionage or sabotage; could fear that a strong position of the foreign company in certain sectors may be used to exert pressure on the host government; or limit sources of supply of critical infrastructure, products or services.

The awareness of threats to essential security interests stemming from economic integration and in particular foreign ownership of certain assets has increased globally. The origin of investments from less than transparent economies or investments made by State-controlled entities play an important role in the risk assessment of open economies in which such investment may take place. Technological change, the vulnerabilities created, transmitted or aggravated by advanced technology, and the importance and use of data for various, including nefarious purposes, have recently attracted particular attention and heightened attention on the security implications of certain investments. A more assertive stance of some countries in global economic and strategic competition has likely also contributed to greater awareness and concerns about countries' interests, modes of operation, and resulting threats to essential security interests that may be associated with international investment.

This awareness is documented by a steep increase in the number of countries that have established or strengthened policies to manage acquisition- or ownership-related risk to their essential security interests. In the past two years, nine out of the world's ten largest economies have taken such policy measures, and many smaller economies have likewise introduced such policies since 2017, many for the first time. As a consequence, since around 2009, the share in global FDI inflows subject to cross-sectoral investment screening to safeguard essential security interests has doubled from around 40% to 80% of total global FDI inflows now (Figure 4.8).

Figure 4.8. Investment policy measures to safeguard essential security interests

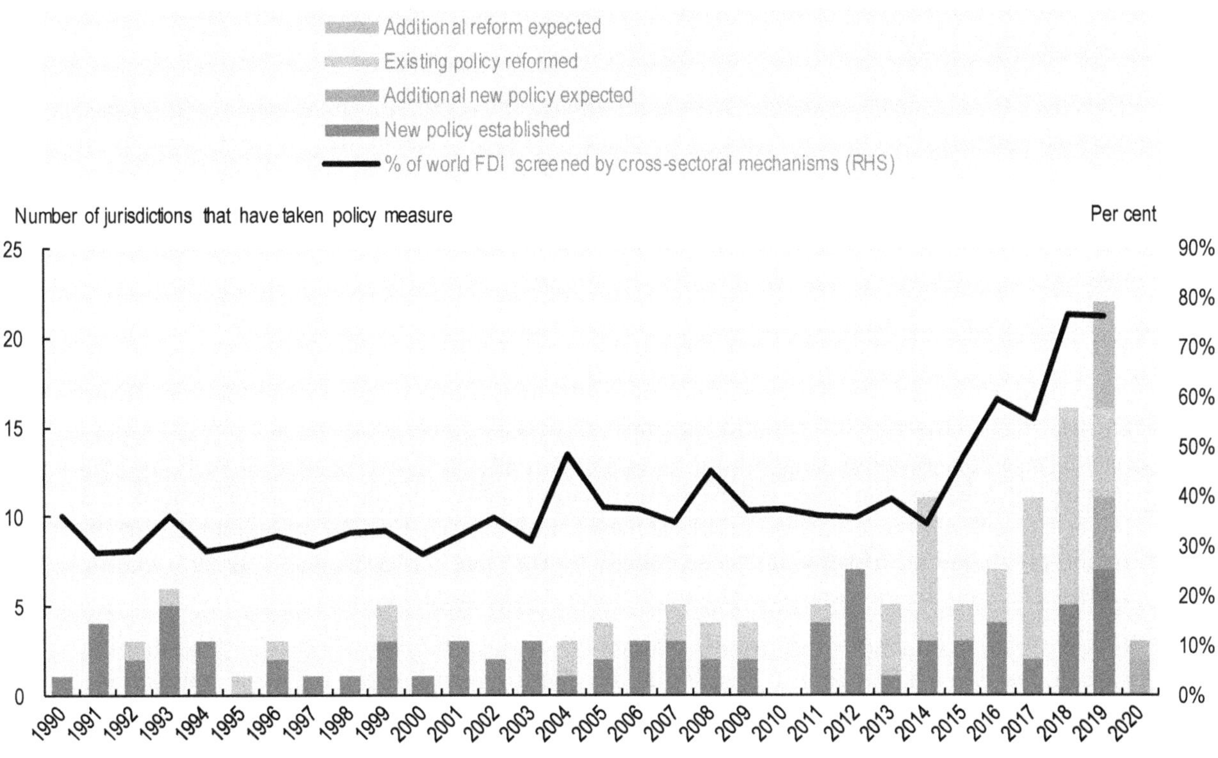

Note: Data for 2018 and 2019 are based on OECD projections.
Source: OECD; FDI data based on IMF and OECD Foreign Direct Investment Statistics database; data for 2018 and 2019 OECD projections.

Countries' policies reveal the perception of threats as they set out the characteristics of transactions that they subject to review. Collectively, policies contain almost as many different acquirer-related aspects as they mention asset-related features, showing that for their perception of risk, the identity and features of the acquirer matters quite a bit. Foreign state ownership of the acquirer specifically is explicitly identified by a number of countries, suggesting a latent distrust about the intentions that foreign governments and their SOEs have when investing abroad. The number of jurisdictions singling out state-ownership explicitly on the face of their policies has grown steadily.

Numerous countries have become increasingly concerned about SOEs motivation for foreign investment. Accordingly, several jurisdictions have revised their respective foreign investment policies by distinguishing between state-owned and private entities. The European Union has also included government control, including through significant government funding, as a factor that EU Member governments may consider in their assessment.[8]

Policies that seek to safeguard countries' essential security interests from threats associated with inward investment are expected to evolve quickly in the next years. A number of jurisdictions – including five of the G7 Members – have signalled their intentions to introduce new policies or are working on reforms to strengthen their mechanisms. Some of these changes are transformational and include controls over outward flows of sensitive technology and permanent surveillance of certain assets to address latent risks of critical infrastructure. There are also plans in some jurisdictions to take critical assets into state-ownership or control them through "golden share" arrangements – an approach reminiscent of a situation that prevailed before large-scale privatisation of such assets in the 1980s that created the exposure in the first place.[9]

4.6. OECD initiatives to ensure a level playing field

The OECD is engaged in numerous activities aimed at improving the governance of SOEs and enhancing the levels of trust in SOEs among competitors and the public. This work centres on encouraging the implementation of the OECD Guidelines on Corporate Governance of State-Owned Enterprises, the world's only internationally endorsed recommendation on good ownership practices by the state. The Guidelines have been publicly endorsed by all OECD member countries as well as Argentina (for an overview, see Box 4.1).

4.6.1. Ensuring competitive neutrality

As previously noted, the state may not only distort the level playing field by favouring entities that it controls, or by allowing those entities to abuse their market power, it may also take actions as a buyer, regulator or supporter that can distort competition in markets in which it does not compete. Where the distortion is caused by governments' actions as a buyer of services these can be addressed by following the OECD recommendation on public procurement. Meanwhile those caused by the state's actions as a regulator can be addressed using the existent OECD Competition Assessment Toolkit.

Further work is therefore currently underway in the OECD, where the Competition Committee is in the process of looking at developing possible principles of competitive neutrality that countries should seek to apply.

4.6.2. Transparency and disclosure

A key aspect of maintaining trust in the level playing field is for economic actors to be subject to high standards of transparency and disclosure as it ensures that owners/shareholders can hold the boards and management accountable; it fosters investor confidence and lowers risk; and ensures a level playing field between market participants.

Box 4.1. OECD Guidelines on Corporate Governance of State-Owned Enterprises

The *OECD Guidelines on Corporate Governance of State-Owned Enterprises* are recommendations to governments on how to ensure that SOEs operate efficiently, transparently and in an accountable manner. These are their main tenets:

- The state should disclose the **rationales for state ownership** to the general public, who are the ultimate owners of SOEs. The purpose of state ownership should be to maximise value for society.
- The **state as an owner** should be professional, transparent and accountable.
- SOEs should compete on a **level playing field** with private companies. State ownership and regulatory functions should be separate to avoid conflicting objectives.
- Non-state **shareholders should have equitable treatment** and equal access to corporate information.
- SOEs should respect stakeholders' rights and implement high standards of **responsible business conduct**.
- SOEs should be subject to the same high standards of **accounting, auditing and disclosure** as listed companies.
- SOE **boards of directors** should have the mandate, autonomy and independence to set enterprise strategy and oversee management, absent of political interference.

Source: Adapted from OECD (2015).

Transparency of course involves corporate financial and non-financial disclosure, but equally important is the quality of auditing which is instrumental in building trust in the disclosed information. The OECD consensus implies that SOEs may be audited by state auditors, but should also be subject to independent external audits. Recently, however, the risk of a weakened competition in an audit sector comprising a shrinking number of global firms, as well as apparent conflicts of interest of auditors who sell a wide array of non-audit services to the corporate sector, have given rise to some concerns in this respect.

Since the adoption of the Guidelines on Corporate Governance of State-Owned Enterprises over a decade ago, many countries around the world have instituted reforms leading to increased transparency in the state-owned enterprise sector, both at the level of individual SOEs and at the level of the state. Heightened disclosure practices have often occurred in tandem with other trends, including the professionalization of the state-ownership function, SOEs' corporatisation and the listing of some SOEs on stock exchanges. In a majority of OECD's member and partner countries annual reporting on SOE portfolios (or at least some aspects of SOE portfolios) are now an enshrined practice (Figure 4.9).

Ensuring adequate transparency and disclosure of the state-owned enterprise sector has gained importance beyond the domestic reform agenda. This is because over the past decade the global economy has witnessed an increase in SOEs' international trade and investment activity, and an increasingly number of SOEs are essentially operating as multinationals. At the international level, recent firm-level analysis confirms that there is still a general lack of information or disclosure by SOEs (OECD, 2019b; Transparency International, 2016), which in turn has contributed to concerns about SOEs perhaps operating abroad according to non-commercial considerations.

Figure 4.9. Regular reporting on SOE portfolios by the state (55 contributing countries)

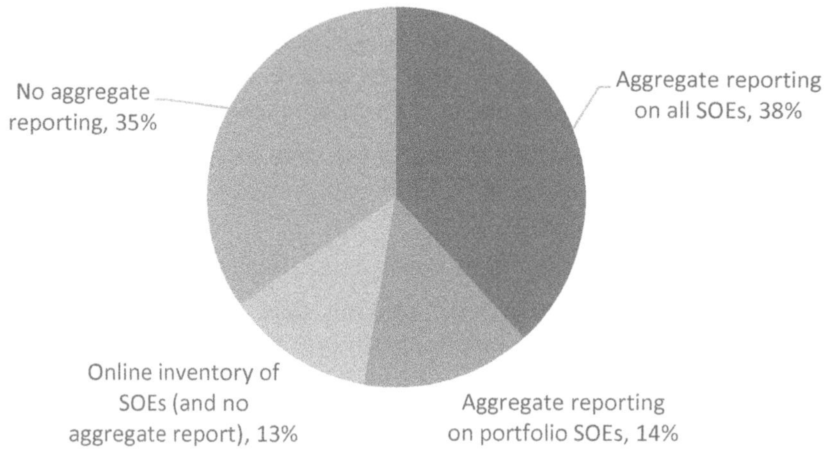

Source: OECD (2018d).

Further OECD initiatives are underway to address these issues. The Working Party on State Ownership and Privatisation Practices will be developing best practices for disclosure by individual SOEs and by their government ownership. In a world where SOEs figure increasingly prominently in debates about international trade and investment, the implementation of such guidance will be an important step toward building trust, at home and abroad.

4.6.3. Fighting corruption

Avoiding corruption in SOEs is primarily the responsibility of the State as an enterprise owner, but at the same time the state cannot be overly intrusive or intervene on an ad-hoc basis without jeopardising the rules of good corporate governance. An active and informed ownership, exercised on a whole-of-government basis in accordance with the OECD Guidelines on Corporate Governance of State-Owned Enterprises, remains essential. Many state owners have clear rules and expectations in place to promote integrity and prevent corruption in their companies.

But more can and should be done. Some of the most problematic cases of SOE corruption have been attributed to a more widespread lack of integrity in the public sector, including among those charged with exercising ownership over the SOEs. It is vitally important for policy makers and high-level public officials to implement high standards of integrity throughout the public sector.

The OECD has adopted a new recommendation, titled "The Anti-Corruption and Integrity Guidelines for State-Owned Enterprises" (OECD, 2019a).[10] These Guidelines are the first international instrument to offer states, in their role as enterprise owners, support in fighting corruption and promoting integrity the enterprises they own (see Box 4.2). They supplement and complement existing global standards providing good practices for fighting corruption and ensuring integrity. Their implementation will be a vital step toward building public trust in SOEs and public officials involved in their operations.

Box 4.2. Main building blocks of the Anti-Corruption and Integrity Guidelines for SOEs

Integrity of the state

- Apply high standards of conduct to those exercising ownership of SOEs on behalf of the general public.
- Establish ownership arrangements that are conducive to integrity.

Ownership and governance

- Ensure clarity in the legal and regulatory framework and in the State's expectations.
- Act as an informed and active owner with regards to integrity in SOEs.

Corruption prevention

- Require adequate mechanisms for addressing risks of corruption.
- Require adoption of high quality integrity mechanisms within SOEs.
- Safeguard the autonomy of SOEs and their decision-making bodies.

Corruption detection and response

- Establish appropriate accountability and review mechanisms for SOEs.
- Taking action and respecting due process for investigations and prosecutions.
- Invite the inputs of civil society, the public, media and the business community.

Source: Adapted from OECD (2019a).

Ensuring national security

The OECD investment policy community hosts inclusive dialogue on acquisition- and ownership-related policies to safeguard essential security interests and their effect on international investment. This dialogue began in 2006 and is being stepped up now to meet the great demand for policy advice. It sensitises governments for the second-order effect that such policies can have on international investment and endeavours to forge consensus on policy disciplines and good practice to complement the 2009 Guidelines for Recipient Country Investment Policies Relating to National Security were a first milestone on this path. Beyond agreed policy disciplines, international cooperation in implementation will become ever more important now that many countries have introduced review mechanisms to manage potential threats. Such cooperation is likely to include harmonisation of standards across countries to provide a coherent signal to enterprises, how they can diminish their risk profile in relation to acquisition- and ownership-related policies to safeguard essential security interests. State-owned enterprises, which are particularly exposed to such policies in some countries, would then be given a clear signal about host government expectations.

4.7. Challenges and outlook

The outlook is for a continued increase in the importance of SOEs in the international economy. It follows from the structurally high growth rates in economies where state ownership is widespread. Many of these countries have privatisation programmes that are reducing the number of SOEs, but their effect is generally outpaced by the volume growth of the enterprises that remain state owned.

This need not give rise to concern. The position of the OECD is that state ownership of commercial firms is not a problem insofar as these firms are held to high standards of governance and transparency, as recommended by several OECD instruments. Decisions by respective governments to retain ownership of certain SOEs probably indicates that these enterprises are expected to act differently from private firms in some circumstances. Even this circumstance is not considered problematic if the "public policy objectives" of these enterprises are publicly disclosed and their costs covered in a transparent fashion. Clarity on when such public policy objectives outweigh competition objectives is also considered useful.

The changing geographic balance of the global SOE landscape may, however, pose a challenge as most of the fastest-growing SOEs are located in countries that are not party to the OECD consensus. These enterprises could be subject to a two-sided "trust deficit", at home when they compete with domestic private firms, and in foreign jurisdictions where these enterprises may be little known or their ownership objectives poorly understood. High standards of governance and transparency should thus apply when SOEs internationalise their activities, thereby deflecting the risk of distorting a different economy where the public policy justifications for the distortions may not exist. The challenge of building trust is increasingly recognised by a growing number of emerging economy governments, some of whom have expressed public commitments to pursuing competitive neutrality and ensuring that SOEs respect the rule of law.

More could be done. The aforementioned OECD initiatives to raise transparency, improve investment regulation related to state ownership and fight corruption in SOEs will all benefit from the active involvement of OECD's partner countries. Engaging in these undertakings can help countries to build confidence at home as well as among their main commercial partners. A multinational effort to build trust in state ownership will be key to safeguarding an open and competitive environment for trade and investment.

Notes

[1] Part of this growth is due to the fact that one SOE that appeared in the 2000 table was split into six, each of which appear separately in the 2017 table.

[2] Source: IJ Global. In this context infrastructure is defined to include power generation and transmission, transportation, and water and sanitation.

[3] For note, leverage is defined in terms of long-term debt, so companies that have amassed large short-term arrears will not necessarily appear as highly leveraged.

[4] See OECD (2018c). This paper defines a state enterprise as an entity where the state has significant control of corporate decisions through full or majority ownership, or a significant minority of voting shares

[5] In this context, the EU has recently adopted a Directive, the objective of which is to ensure that competition agencies across Europe have the guarantees of independence, resources, and enforcement and fining powers necessary to apply competition law effectively, http://data.europa.eu/eli/dir/2019/1/oj.

[6] The OECD Foreign Bribery Report (2014) found that 27% of foreign bribery cases concluded between 1999 and 2014 were destined for officials of SOEs (as compared to other public officials), amounting to 80% of the total value of bribes offered, promised or given.

[7] An alternative explanation could be that a number of SOEs are legally or politically required to be active in certain economic sectors, which renders them incapable of ceding operations even if they do have concerns about compliance risk.

[8] Regulation (EU) 2019/452 of the European Parliament and of the Council of 19 March 2019 establishing a framework for the screening of foreign direct investments into the Union, http://data.europa.eu/eli/reg/2019/452/oj.

[9] More details on current and emerging trends in acquisition-and ownership-related policies to safeguard essential security interests are set out in a research note by the OECD Secretariat of March 2019, www.oecd.org/investment/Current-and-emerging-trends-2019.pdf.

[10] This work is being led by the Working Party on State Ownership and Privatisation Practices, with the cooperation of the Working Group on Bribery and the Working Party of Senior Public Integrity Officials.

References

Cannizzaro, Anthony P. and Robert J. Weiner, "State Ownership and Transparency in Foreign Direct Investment: Loose-Lipped Leviathan?"I IEP-WP-2017-18, September 2017, *Institute for International Economic Policy Working Paper Series*.

Edelman (2018), *2018 Edelman Trust Barometer*, www.edelman.com/research/2018-edelman-trust-barometer.

OECD (2019a), *Guidelines on Anti-Corruption and Integrity in State-Owned Enterprises*, www.oecd.org/corporate/oecd-guidelines-anti-corruption-integrity-state-owned-enterprises.htm.

OECD (2019b), "Measuring distortions in international markets: the aluminium value chain", *OECD Trade Policy Papers,* No. 218, OECD Publishing, Paris http://dx.doi.org/10.1787/c82911ab-en

OECD (2018a), *State-Owned Enterprises and Corruption: What Are the Risks and What Can Be Done?*, OECD Publishing, Paris, https://doi.org/10.1787/9789264303058-en

OECD (2018b), *Integrity for Good Governance in Latin America and the Caribbean: From Commitments to Action*, OECD Publishing, Paris, https://doi.org/10.1787/9789264201866-en.

OECD (2018c), "State enterprises in the steel sector", *OECD Science, Technology and Industry Policy Papers, No. 53*, OECD Publishing, Paris, https://doi.org/10.1787/2a8ad9cd-en .

OECD (2018d), *Ownership and Governance of State-Owned Enterprises: A Compendium of National Practices*, www.oecd.org/corporate/Ownership-and-Governance-of-State-Owned-Enterprises-A-Compendium-of-National-Practices.pdf.

OECD (2017), *The Size and Sectoral Distribution of State-Owned Enterprises,* OECD Publishing, Paris, https://dx.doi.org/10.1787/9789264280663-en.

OECD (2016a), *Broadening the Ownership of State-Owned Enterprises: A Comparison of Governance Practices,* OECD Publishing, Paris, https://doi.org/10.1787/9789264244603-en.

OECD (2016b), *State-Owned Enterprises as Global Competitors: A Challenge or an Opportunity?*, OECD Publishing, Paris, https://doi.org/10.1787/9789264262096-en.

OECD (2015a), *OECD Guidelines on Corporate Governance of State-Owned Enterprises*, OECD Publishing, Paris, http://dx.doi.org/10.1787/9789264244160-en.

OECD (2015b), "Discussion of Competitive Neutrality, mimeo (unpublished).

OECD (2014), *OECD Foreign Bribery Report: An Analysis of the Crime of Bribery of Foreign Public Officials*, OECD Publishing, Paris, www.oecd.org/corruption/oecd-foreign-bribery-report-9789264226616-en.htm.

Shima, Y. (2015), "The Policy Landscape for International Investment by Government-controlled Investors: A Fact Finding Survey", *OECD Working Paper on International Investment* 2015/01, http://dx.doi.org/10.1787/5js7svp0jkns-en.

Sultan Balbuena, S. (2016), "Concerns Related to the Internationalisation of State-Owned Enterprises: Perspectives from regulators, government owners and the broader business community", *OECD Corporate Governance Working Papers,* No. 19, OECD Publishing, Paris. http://dx.doi.org/10.1787/5jm0xvx0b223-en.

Telia (2017), "Telia Company reaches a global settlement with the authorities regarding Uzbekistan investigation", www.teliacompany.com/en/news/press-releases/2017/9/telia-company-reaches-a-global-settlement-with-the-authorities-regarding-uzbekistan-investigation/.

Transparency International (2016), *Transparency in corporate reporting: assessing emerging market multinationals*, www.transparency.org/whatwedo/publication/transparency_in_corporate_reporting_assessing_emerging_market_multinat.

Chapter 5. Trust and online markets

Online markets offer a host of benefits for consumers through innovative and low-cost products. However, online markets can only fulfil their potential if they benefit from consumer trust. Where product information is hard to obtain and assess, markets may not respond to consumer needs. Consumers may be forced to rely on imprecise indicators of quality—such as brand names—to establish trust. This, in turn, limits firms' incentives to improve their offering and deters new entrants. In other cases, consumers may be deterred from using online markets altogether. Establishing an environment of trust in online markets requires multidisciplinary (and often cross-border) approaches from authorities charged with ensuring fair competition, consumer protection, and data protection, as well as other regulators. This chapter considers the benefits and risks associated with online markets from the perspective of trust.

5.1. Introduction

Technological changes are reshaping the functioning of many markets and introducing new ones. Online markets[1] for products offered to final consumers are growing in importance, and have become a key sector of the global economy today (OECD, 2012, p. 5). Activity in these markets, broadly termed e-commerce,[2] has grown significantly, with total worldwide online retail sales increasing from 1.336 trillion US dollars in 2014 to 2.304 trillion US dollars in 2017 (Statista, 2019a). This trend in transaction value is expected to continue, while the number of people around the world buying online is forecast to increase from 1.66 billion in 2016 to over 2.14 billion in 2021 (Statista, 2019b). The digital transformation, and its role in reshaping traditional markets, is here to stay.

Figure 5.1. Total worldwide e-commerce sales (USD billions), 2014-2021

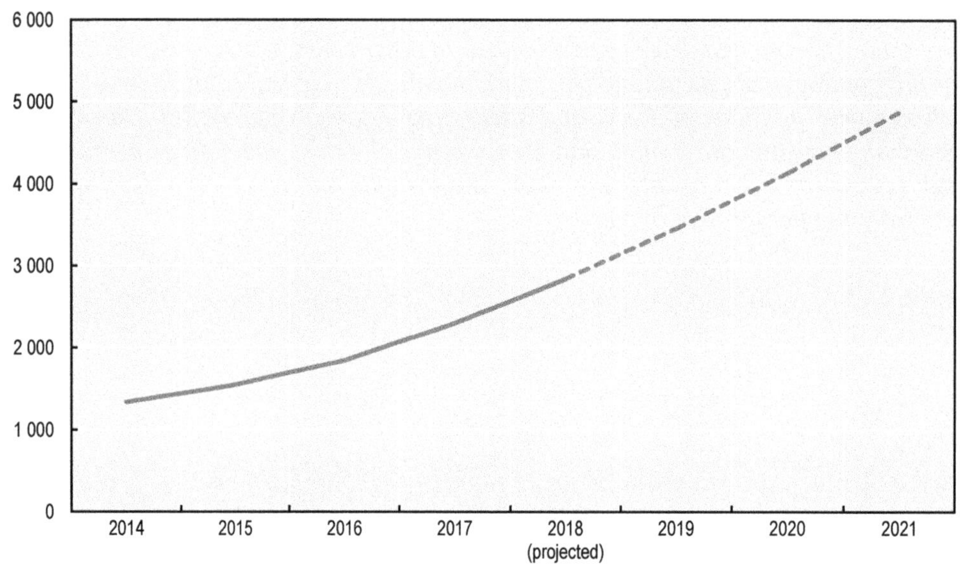

Source: Statista (2019a).

This digital transformation has fundamentally changed how many consumers make purchases and acquire information about products. Consumers can shop from suppliers located anywhere in the world, with only limited constraints due to logistics or regulation. They can also benefit from increased transparency, which enhances choice and may reduce transaction costs considerably (Friederiszick, Glowicka 2016, p. 43).

Online markets do not only allow consumers to shop online for products that they would previously have only found in brick-and-mortar shops, but also to benefit from the creation of new business models and the development of new products. One example is the growth of businesses that offer products at a price of zero in exchange for consumer data or attention to advertising. This latter type of business model existed before the digital economy, and it is typical of the radio, television and newspaper industries. However, the scale at which it occurs in the new digital era and the amount of innovative products that it is generating is different: nowadays, seven out of the ten largest global companies operating in digital markets provide zero-price products (PwC, 2018).

With these benefits also come some challenges. The availability of information, through consumer reviews and rating systems, price comparison websites, or price transparency between retailers, generally thought to facilitate decision-making, could in some cases be counterproductive. For example, fake or misleading consumer reviews, price comparison websites, and rating systems may hamper consumers' ability to select the product that is right for them (OECD, 2019a). In addition, greater transparency in pricing may be used by suppliers to limit price competition (through resale price maintenance policies imposed on retailers), or to collude among themselves (OECD, 2018a, p. 10).

Further, while consumers can benefit from customised services obtained for a price of zero in exchange for their data, these new business models have raised some privacy and consumer protection concerns to which markets may not be responsive (Stucke and Grunes, 2016, pp. 56-57). In particular, while data is a key unit of exchange in online services, consumers do not appear to consider this in their decision-making, and are in any event given few if any opportunities to make meaningful choices about the terms of this exchange. Limited awareness of how much of their data is collected, how it will be used (e.g. to target advertising or sell to third parties), and the implications of this use, creates significant risks for consumers as well.

Due to these risks and challenges, the role of trust in online markets is particularly important. As with any market, consumers must trust that a product or service provider will fulfil its obligation for the market to function properly. However, with respect to online transactions involving a range of unseen variables, ranging from algorithms that generate personalised pricing, to data collection with privacy implications, trust takes on a new importance in e-commerce. In other words, consumers must have confidence that online markets will develop to bring them a greater range of services in an effective manner and that they will not be exploited when concluding transactions online.

For the purposes of this Chapter, trust in online markets can be defined as the willingness of an online consumer, in the presence of uncertainty, to take the risk of entering into a transaction with an online provider of goods or services.[3] A similar definition is proposed by the OECD: *"From an individuals' point of view, trust in the digital age is about the willingness to risk time, money, and disclosure of personal data to engage in commercial and social activities, and to become vulnerable if a purchase goes wrong or if their data are stolen or if they are used to monitor their behaviour, to discriminate against them or to violate their privacy"* (2019, p. 120).

Uncertainty is a key element of online transactions requiring consumer trust. Consumers may experience uncertainty with respect to the integrity of online transaction systems (such as security breaches in data exchanges or errors in the processing of the transaction) and regarding the behaviour of the players involved (such as the willingness of the supplier to provide a product of quality) (Grabner-Kraeuter, 2002, p. 45). While legal frameworks provide some protection in relation to some aspects of the online transaction, some consumers may be limited in their ability to verify *ex ante* or monitor throughout the transaction the reliability of the supplier. As Head and Hassanein put it: *"Consumers may at first feel a sense of chaos in the e-commerce market, as they fear that their personal information may be stolen due to unreliable security and that online businesses may be fraudulent [...] Trust also involves vulnerability. When people trust they expose themselves to risk."* (2001, pp. 11-12).

Given this element of uncertainty and risk, trust is required, first, for consumers to engage in online transactions and to have confidence that online providers are providing complete and accurate information on the characteristics of their products or services, and will fulfil the obligations they undertake.[4] Second, market participants must trust that unlawful behaviour in these markets, such as misleading, fraudulent or abusive conduct, has a high probability of being detected and punished and that online transactions do not create cybersecurity risks. In addition, society at large expects that online markets are subject to compliance with competition law, data protection, consumer protection and financial regulations. Similarly, both law enforcement authorities and market participants are expected to behave with integrity and enforce or comply with the law. Trust is therefore essential in numerous contexts to support the development of online markets, and their efficient functioning.

While consumers are the most immediately impacted by the trustworthiness of online markets (referred to in other chapters as the trust stakeholder), an insufficient level of trust in a market can have wider implications. For example, SMEs and firms more generally rely on consumer trust to be able to sell their products and services online. Third-parties such as online advertisers and data acquirers also need to be trusted by consumers before establishing of a commercial relationship.

So trust in online markets is crucial in order to create a supportive environment for commerce, but it should not be excessive, i.e. so high that consumers do not critically engage with the information presented to them regarding products or services online. In both cases, the ability of markets to operate competitively and therefore efficiently may be impaired, with significant implications for consumers and economic growth more broadly. Blind trust, defined as "trust in situations that most people would agree do not warrant trust" (Mayer et al., 1995, p. 715) and that may allow exploitation, must be distinguished from informed trust. Vulnerable consumers, who may not have enough information or enough choice, are susceptible to firm misconduct, or at the very least getting a bad deal, if they are blindly trusting in online markets.

No single policy instrument is sufficient to ensure that online markets reach their potential in terms of benefits for consumers. In particular, for consumers to be able to have informed trust in online markets, they must (1) be confident that the boundaries of firm misconduct are clearly-defined and actively enforced, and (2) benefit from enough information and meaningful opportunities to make decisions and get the best deal possible, over and above the minimum legal standards for online products. Competition, consumer protection, data protection and sector regulators all have a role to play, in terms of enforcement, consumer advocacy, and working with policymakers, to promote informed trust.

The structure of this Chapter is as follows:

- Section 2 addresses the reasons why trust plays a prominent role in online markets.
- Section 3 illustrates the potential risks of a loss of trust or of the existence of too much trust in online markets.
- Section 4 identifies the policies that are required to promote an optimal level of informed trust in online markets.

5.2. The role of trust in online markets

As noted above, consumers in online markets face substantial uncertainty, including an inability to inspect physical products before using them, risks of payment methods being compromised, potential privacy violations, and the potential for fraudulent conduct, among others. Thus, trust is crucial for these markets. A 2016 consumer survey conducted by the OECD demonstrated the importance of trust in the minds of digital consumers, especially the role of digital platforms, legal protections, and access to ratings and reviews in promoting that trust (see the "Trust in Peer Platform Markets" report, OECD, 2016b).

Trust may be a particularly important factor for online businesses relying on data collection. A 2012 study found that over 50% of the participants ranked trusting businesses as the most important driver of their willingness to share their data, while over 30% of them agreed that they assigned importance to having previously purchased from a certain brand or business. The study concludes that *"businesses have an obligation to ensure that their brand is trusted by the consumer. If it is not, then the consumer will not feel comfortable in entering into a commercial relationship which requires them to divulge personal data"* (DMA, 2012, p. 16).

The presence of trust is all the more fundamental for the functioning of online markets due to the fact that, in some cases, the interaction between the players involves a considerable divergence of interests between users, suppliers, advertisers and data brokers that operate in them. This principal agent problem may negatively impact consumer trust and either discourage consumers from entering the market or make them too confident on the bona fide of the other players involved.

Misaligned incentives could be found in search engine markets, for instance, where the interest of consumers in terms of accuracy of results may conflict with the supplier's desire to earn revenue by promoting advertiser websites. This in turn may clash with the advertisers' interest to reach users in a more targeted and accurate way (Stucke and Ezrachi, 2016, p. 92).

Therefore, without a desirable degree of trust, online markets are unlikely to work efficiently and maximise consumer welfare. The misalignment of incentives is likely to originate or be exacerbated by other issues, such as information asymmetries, consumers inertia, and consumer behavioural biases that can emerge in online markets. Each of these issues and its implications for consumers' trust are discussed in detail below.

5.2.1. Information asymmetries

Online markets involve considerable information asymmetries between online providers and consumers. For example, some products sold online are considered experience goods or credence goods, i.e. products whose quality can only be evaluated after they are used, or cannot be observed at all (OECD, 2010, pp. 32-33; OECD, 2018b, p. 24). This means that their level of quality may be very difficult to assess for consumers.

When buying physical goods online, one major difficulty that consumers may encounter is the inability to check the merchandise in advance. In addition, differences in consumer protection laws between countries may constitute an important barrier to cross-border sales. There can also be uncertainty about the reliability of the online sellers, especially when it is not an established brand.

Further, consumers face difficulties in understanding the terms of exchange for transactions in which the price is zero, and the consumer instead provides a non-monetary asset, such as access to their data or their attention to advertising. The limits associated with collecting, analysing and applying information about the transaction, the quality of the good or service, and the terms of use in online markets create opportunities for the exploitation of consumers (Acquisti et al., 2015). Pricing algorithms that use data on a consumer's characteristics to develop personalised prices have also become an area of consumer concern (OECD, 2018d).

In order to make informed purchasing decisions when undertaking e-commerce transactions, consumers need relevant and accurate information concerning goods and services and the vendors who are supplying them. Imperfect information may either foster blind trust or reduce trust on the part of consumers, who may overestimate the value of the online good or service and underestimate that of their privacy or of the data exchanged or vice versa. They may therefore decide whether to engage in an online transaction based on an incomplete cost-benefit analysis. In a 2015 Report by the UK competition authority, it emerged that *"[s]ome consumers identify a 'value exchange' from sharing data, but most feel they lack information on how they benefit and perceive firms benefit more that they do"* (CMA, 2015, p. 106). Another US study conducted in 2015 showed that the vast majority of the respondents (91%) disagreed that: *"[i]f companies give me a discount, it is a fair exchange for them to collect information about me without my knowing"* (Turow et al., 2015, p. 4).

A number of studies also highlight the low level of consumer awareness with regard to data collection. One study shows that, even when available to consumers, the magnitude of information makes it impossible in practice to process it: internet users would need to devote an average of 244 hours per year to consulting terms and conditions of the websites they navigate (McDonald and Cranor, 2008). And even when provided with full information, consumers often find the explanations provided to them unintelligible. Online privacy policy notices may not be sufficient to protect privacy or serve as an effective tool to inform consumers. As noted in a US 2014 Report, *"[n]otice and consent creates a non-level playing field in the implicit privacy negotiation between provider and user. The provider offers a complex, take-it-or-leave-it set of terms, while the user, in practice, can allocate only a few seconds to evaluating the offer. This is a kind of market failure".*[5]

These studies suggest that many consumers' choices in online markets are not an expression of their preferences and of the minimal value they assign to their own data and their privacy, but may be the result of a lack of understanding of the implications of their online activity (Stucke and Grunes, 2016, pp. 58-61), or a limited ability to influence the terms (Ben-Shahar, 2008). The intangibility of the harm caused by a privacy violation and the opaqueness of the terms of the trade-off are often at the origin of inertia (Acquisti et al., 2015, pp. 509-510) that pushes consumers to either blindly trust the online providers, or avoid purchasing altogether.

Aggravating information asymmetries is the risk that online consumers may experience the problem of "information overload" (OECD, 2018e). Consumers may be unable to process all of the information provided to them, for example as can be the case with terms and conditions regarding the collection of personal data.

When generally unaware or overwhelmed, consumers are unlikely to take actions that reflect their desire for better privacy or data protection. But when provided with clearer information, consumers in some cases seem more prone to engage in a cost-benefit evaluation and to prefer options offering increased privacy protection. One experiment conducted in 2011 asked participants to use an especially created search engine to purchase specific products. At first, the search engine only provided access to the sellers' websites and price information and the main driver of participants' purchasing decisions was price. When the search engine displayed additional clear and easily accessible information about privacy protection, most participants opted to pay a higher price to buy from the sellers affording a higher level of privacy protection (Tsai et al., 2011).

5.2.2. Consumer behavioural biases

In addition to information asymmetry issues, additional demand side problems arise in online markets from some consumer behavioural biases. These biases may "push" consumers to implicitly trust a transaction when caution may be warranted, preventing fulsome decision-making and creating risks of exploitative conduct. These and other biases are explored in detail in the OECD Digital Working Paper on "Improving Online Disclosures with Behavioural Insights" (OECD, 2018e).

The free effect

One potential phenomenon identified in some studies is the "free effect", where consumers disproportionately value a price of zero at the expense of all other determinants of quality (see, for instance, Shampan'er and Ariely, 2016). Given that many product characteristics, such as consumer data protection, are complex and involve substantial information asymmetries, the impact of the free effect may be particularly acute.

One example is the introduction by Amazon of free shipping in part of Europe. At the time of its adoption, the free shipping offer was not implemented in France due to a programming error. In France, the price of shipping was reduced, but remained positive at 1 French Franc, a minimal amount. While orders skyrocketed in countries where the shipping was free, in France the impact of the shipping cost reduction was negligible (Shampan'er et al., 2007, p. 756).

A zero price could have the powerful effect of leading consumers to implicitly trust an online provider, without giving adequate consideration to the value of the 'exchanged good', such as, for instance, their privacy or data protection. Moreover, firms can use the free effect to their benefit in multi-product offers to block entry of new competitors or to drive out of the market the existing ones, ultimately to the detriment of consumers.

The privacy paradox

While consumers report valuing privacy in a range of surveys, there is mixed evidence regarding whether consumers incorporate these concerns in their behaviour. This phenomenon is known as the "privacy paradox". In particular, consumer purchasing behaviour does not always appear to take account of privacy considerations.

Although consumers seem to have generally become increasingly concerned about how their data is collected and used when accessing online services, they continue to use those services. For example, a US survey revealed that the vast majority of the respondents felt that consumers have lost control over how firms' collect and use personal data, and 80% of those who are active on social networks are concerned about the fact that third parties may have access to the data they share. According to a 2014 survey on internet security and trust, 64% of respondents admitted to being more concerned about privacy in 2014 than they were in the previous year (OECD, 2017a, p. 248). A Eurobarometer report on cybersecurity showed that the main worries of online consumers in the EU are misuse of personal data and the security of online payments (European Commission, 2015). One recurrent issue users mention in relation to e-commerce, as opposed to traditional businesses, is that they *"may not trust Internet transactions more generally"* (OECD, 2017a, p. 208). According to a survey conducted in the United States in 2017, 69% of participants think that there are high risks of hacks and cyberattacks and only 25% of them consider that companies handle personal data in a responsible way. Just 10% of respondents expressed the view that they have full control over their personal data. When asked which types of businesses the participants trusted most, only 13% indicated online retailers and 6% social media.

In spite of these concerns, however, consumers continue to purchase online products and services. The firms providing these services have thrived in recent years and many are rapidly growing. While in 1995, the largest firms in online markets were Internet service providers, in 2017 the biggest players were online platforms, with Google, Amazon, Facebook, Alibaba, and Uber entering the top 15 (OECD, 2017a, p. 208).

Although evidence is mixed, according to some studies consumers would be willing to pay at least a minimal amount to have access to services guaranteeing more privacy (OECD, 2018b, pp. 26-27). One potential explanation of why consumers' fears may not translate into action is examined in the Section below.

Inertia and the status quo

An important distortion that prevent consumers' preference from being reflected in online market is inertia. Consumers may experience a sense of powerlessness in relation to their privacy and data protection online. In one survey, while most of consumers indicated that they would like to do more to protect their privacy online, only *"24% of adults 'agree' or 'strongly agree' with the statement that: 'It is easy for me to be anonymous when I am online'"* (Madden, 2014). Consumers are also often strongly influenced by default options, showing a lack of propensity to change the status quo (OECD, 2010, pp. 46-47). The commercial importance of the status quo and the lack of consumers' response are demonstrated by the value business place in being the default option, such as, for instance, when search engines compete to be the default choice in a browser (Stucke and Grunes, 2016, p. 121).

5.3. Businesses may therefore have opportunities to exploit consumer inertia

For example, a practice called "shrouding" consists of making the disclosure of terms and conditions for online transactions purposely complex so as to prevent consumers from engaging meaningfully with the information (Gabaix and Laibson, 2005, pp. 2-3 and 25). In addition, to the extent that consumers are able to change their privacy settings, businesses may set the default at a relatively high level of personal data disclosure and sharing, taking advantage of status quo biases (see, for instance, OECD, 2019c, p.29). The Risk of a Loss or an Excess of Trust in Online Markets.

The market characteristics identified above may affect trust in online markets. As a result, they may opt not to participate in these markets or, as seems to be the case in at least some markets, they may choose to purchase online products despite a lack of trust. The latter decision could be the result of 'blind' or 'implicit' trust on the part of consumers, for instance when they prefer to skip reading complicated privacy policies when accessing free services. A lack of trust may therefore either limit the broad economic and consumer welfare benefits of online markets, or it may expose consumers to firm misconduct while limiting competition.

5.3.1. The risk of a loss of trust in online markets

As described in Section 2, the functioning of online markets for consumer goods and services hinges upon trust. Even firms that have not engaged in misconduct could be harmed by a general distrust of online markets. Such an outcome could limit the further adoption of e-commerce, since there is still room to grow: in 2014, three quarters of consumers in the OECD countries went online, but only about 50% of them shopped via the internet (OECD, 2017b, p. 24). More seriously, a sudden loss of trust in response to a prominent incident could cause existing consumers to withdraw from online markets. The consequences may be particularly serious for small- and medium-sized businesses (see, for example, OECD, 2019d, p. 158). Thus, without trust, the growth and adoption of new digital markets may be at risk, limiting the ability of these markets to reach their potential in contributing to economic growth and consumer welfare.

Fears of personal data breaches, concerns relating to the complexity of terms and conditions in online purchases or, more generally, the difficulties connected to product liability and consumer guarantees may affect the willingness of consumers to share their data and engage in a transaction (OECD, 2017b, p. 24). For example, around 15% of internet users in the EU28 abstained from purchasing online on account of concerns regarding the delivery or the return of the good in 2017 (OECD, 2019b, p. 126).

Businesses are also exposed to concerns about trust when they make purchases in online markets. Uncertainties about the security of data storage and processing may prevent firms from adopting cloud computing solutions and other digital tools. Data show that SME cloud computing services are underused and that SMEs are not fully informed or fully equipped to manage privacy and security threats (OECD, 2017b, p. 24).

Concerns about trust and the risks of losing it are recognised by at least some digital firms. Consumer surveys corroborate this: in a survey conducted in the United States in 2017, the vast majority of participants indicated they would *"not do business with a company if they had concerns about its security practices"* (see PwC, 2017 and Figure 5.2).

Figure 5.2. Results of a survey of US consumers on trust and data security

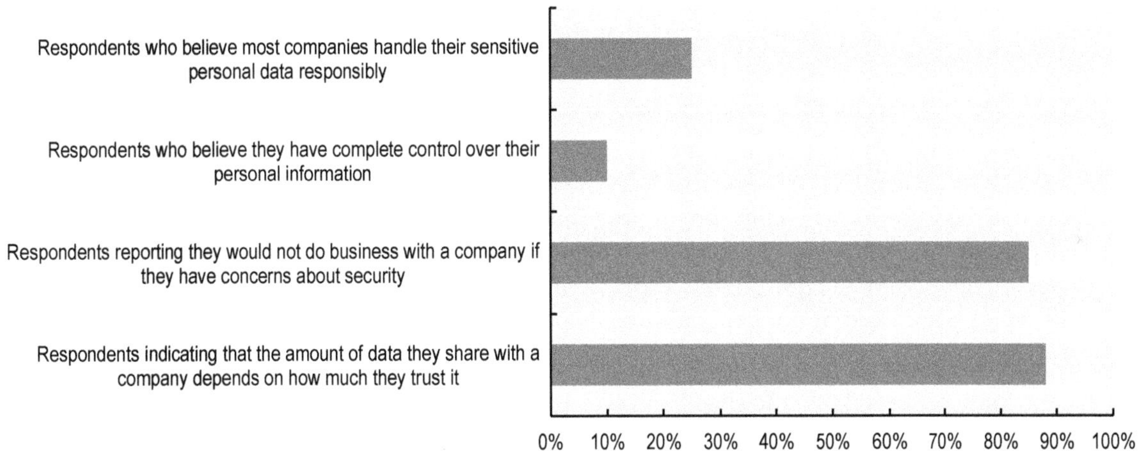

Note: Based on a nationally representative sample of 2 000 Americans surveyed through online survey and virtual interviews.
Source: PwC (2017).

5.3.2. The risk of an excess of trust in online markets

An excess of trust may also be problematic in online markets. If consumers are not actively engaged in assessing the online products they use, for example in terms of privacy and data security, advertising content or ease of switching, they are in essence implicitly trusting the firms that supply these products. This is not to say that consumers are at fault, since they may not be supplied with enough accurate information, available information may be difficult to understand, and alternative products may be scarce. While disengagement in these cases is an understandable response, it can contribute to a vicious cycle, as it will limit the ability of competition to improve the terms offered to consumers while increasing risks of misleading, fraudulent or abusive conduct.

As mentioned above, consumer data plays a fundamental role in many online markets. The complexity of assessing data collection and usage for consumers can, however, be insurmountable. Firms themselves may not know at the time of its collection how a data point will be used, what datasets it will be combined with, who it will be shared with, and whether it can be fully anonymised (or later associated with an individual). Consumers facing this complexity, without the ability to assess the implications of the collection of their data, often choose the blind trust approach of accepting the terms and conditions. They may later fall victim to poor data protection, vague data governance policies, or unexpected consequences such as the use of their data to develop a personalised price.

Another particular risk that may arise in online markets is the manipulation of available information. For example, price comparison websites can have a significant impact on the competitiveness of the market. They have the potential to reduce search, switching and transaction costs for consumers, facilitate market entry and growth, and increase supplier competition. The benefits of digital comparison tools are only felt, however, if they are trustworthy. A recent study by the UK Competition and Markets Authority found that consumers may lack the ability to assess whether these tools are unbiased and may not have a sufficient level of understanding of how they work (CMA, 2017a, p. 70). Some individuals were unaware of the fact that the tools are offered by commercial companies for profit, in some cases as a marketing service for suppliers, and a majority assumed that they are verified and approved by some regulators before going online. In addition, about one third of the respondents admitted that they did not know if digital comparison tools provided full market coverage, i.e. listing of all existing suppliers, when often it is not the case (CMA, 2017b, p. 20).

Another example of the potential inefficiencies brought about by an excess of trust is that of consumer reviews. On the one hand, online reviews may significantly affect consumers' decision-making and, when they are honest, they support trust in online markets, increasing transparency and allowing consumers' to benefit from their peers' perspective on some of the aforementioned uncontrollable aspects of the transaction, such as the risk of non-delivery of goods and of not being able to inspect the goods in advance.

On the other hand, concerns may be raised by the proliferation of misleading reviews. A recent study observed that the speed and rate at which some products sold on Amazon.com are positively reviewed by consumers may be evidence of artificial reviews. According to ReviewMeta, in June, July and August 2017 there was a steep drop in the average review weight, which may suggest that fraudulent reviews were being posted to increase the visibility of certain products. Amazon took steps to ban incentivised reviews and filed lawsuits against more than 1000 individuals and organisations on grounds of review abuse (Woollacott, 2017). Similarly, suspicions arose in relation to the reliability of some TripAdvisor reviews after positive reviews appeared in relation to non-existing restaurants. The Italian competition authority fined the website for improper business practices in 2014, after complaints that the website's content was described as authentic while false reviews had appeared on it.[6] More recently, the Australian competition authority fined Meriton for having manipulated TripAdvisor's reviews of its properties,[7] and an Italian court sentenced to 9 months in prison an individual who sold fake hotel reviews with a false identity.[8] The UK Competition and Market Authority also took action against online fake reviews,[9] and is currently investigating paid for endorsement on social media platforms that influences consumers' buying decisions.[10]

5.4. A policy agenda for trust in digital markets

Trust, and specifically the right amount of informed trust, is crucial for the functioning of online markets. However, as noted above, in some cases consumers have no choice but to blindly trust firms, as they are not given the information or meaningful choices to make an informed decision about the online products they obtain. Other consumers have opted not to use online markets because of a lack of trust. A particularly complex problem may arise, in certain cases, in correctly establishing and attributing the liability for a specific breach of trust in online markets. The rules of allocation of responsibility may vary from country to country (Chun, 2019). Regulation plays a fundamental role in determining who may be responsible for an infringement and in ensuring that adequate mechanisms for redress exist. Policy action can establish and promote informed trust in online markets.

First, consumer and data protection policies can establish minimum acceptable standards, for example with respect to product returns, data governance, and clarity in contractual terms, among others (see OECD, 2018f). These measures require careful design to avoid unintended consequences that stifle innovation and competition – well-crafted approaches can in fact stimulate competition in areas important to consumers, such as privacy. At the same time, enforcement action under existing consumer protection legislation can protect consumers from deceptive, misleading, or fraudulent commercial practices.

Competition authorities can also play an active role in promoting a procompetitive level of trust in online markets. Vigilant enforcement will play a role, but authorities must also use their broader policy toolkit to help inform consumers and provide input on new measures by consumer and data protection authorities. They must also be vocal about making clear that competition is an essential feature of online markets that consumers can trust.

This is borne out by the fact that private initiatives and new business models are already being introduced to bridge some information asymmetries and promote consumer trust. These include, for instance, the development of anonymised features of online digital services, initiatives to enable data portability, voluntary submission to certification schemes, use of third party validated rating and review features, adoption of more favourable data protection or privacy protection terms and conditions, the use of distributed ledger technology or a premium version of a service that guarantees a higher level of privacy protection. It should be noted that this latter option should be intended as offering varied level of privacy above a certain minimum standard of privacy, guaranteed to all consumers.

One recent example is the Tide Foundation, which is using blockchain technology to limit access to consumers' data through encryption, allowing access only to the individual to which the data belong (Shapiro, 2018). This technology would make it possible for businesses intending to target advertisements to a certain category of consumers to use the Tide platform to request data access from users themselves. A choice would then be given to the consumers as to whether to accept to share their data and receive a fair compensation for their use, or to deny approval.

Another example of a private initiative that is not focused on the development of new technologies but on the involvement of consumers to regain trust is the one adopted by TripAdvisor to stop fake reviews. TripAdvisor allows users to mark with a grey flag reviews that seem suspicious or in violation of the website's guidelines.[11] Some websites, such as Fakespot.com and Reviewmeta.com, apply algorithms to analyse reviews and identify unreliable ones.

Further progress in this regard can be encouraged though the competition policy, consumer protection policy, data protection policy, financial consumer protection policy and potential regulatory measures explored below.

5.4.1. Consumer and data protection regulation

A prerequisite for the proper functioning of online markets in a way that engenders consumer trust is the enforcement of consumer protection law. In particular, provisions regarding deceptive advertising, disclosure, product safety, and fraud must be vigilantly applied in online markets. It should be emphasised that a price of zero is generally not a barrier to the legal applicability of these laws (OECD, 2018b).

Box 5.1. The EU General Data Protection Regulation

The General Data Protection Regulation (GDPR), entered into force on 25th May 2018, is aimed at providing individuals a consistent level of data protection throughout the EU. The personal data protected by the Regulation are "*any information relating to an identified or identifiable natural person*", while processing activity is defined as "*any operation or set of operations which is performed on personal data or on sets of personal data, whether or not by automated means, such as collection, recording, organisation, structuring, storage, adaptation or alteration, retrieval, consultation, use, disclosure by transmission, dissemination or otherwise making available, alignment or combination, restriction, erasure or destruction*" (Article 4).

The GDPR strengthened, in particular, the individuals' right to switching by expressly recognising the right to:

- receive the personal data that have been provided to a natural or legal person "in a structured, commonly used and machine-readable format";
- provide another natural or legal person with those data without hindrance from the former data controller; or
- request that personal data are sent directly from one natural or legal person to the other, if practically possible (Article 20).

In addition to granting the right to portability, this Regulation provides that individuals can ask their data controller to indicate what personal data they hold and ask for their deletion (Article 15 and Article 17). It also redefines the conditions for the provision of consent by individuals, prohibiting default opt-out options, pre-ticked boxes and unclear language (Article 7).

The Regulation provides for the application of significant administrative fines of up to 20 million Euros or, for undertakings, 4% of annual global turnover for the most serious infringements (Article 83).

However, adapting existing consumer protection policies to novel types of digital products will be a challenge. Consumer redress mechanisms may not easily match the cross-border nature of online transactions. Applying consumer protection law to peer-to-peer transaction platforms may not be straightforward (see OECD, 2016b). Enforcing consumer protection rules may also involve some unique challenges. The OECD Recommendation on Ecommerce

(OECD, 2016a), and the OECD Toolkit for Protecting Digital Consumers (OECD, 2018f) provide guidance in addressing these and other challenges. In the financial sector, additional consumer protection strategies have been identified by the G20-OECD Task Force on Consumer Protection, including with respect to financial literacy.[12]

The protection of personal data and privacy are also crucial for the functioning of online markets (OECD, 2018b, pp. 96-97). Rules regarding the disclosure of data collection and use, as well as the data protection responsibilities that are triggered when a firm collects data, are coming into increasing focus. Beyond these fundamental protections, an additional right being implemented by data protection regulators to help increase consumer choices and enable new entry into digital markets is data portability.[13] This measure recognises that limited portability constitutes a significant switching cost for consumers, limiting their ability to get the best deal possible. For example, in the EU, the consumer right to data portability was recently granted by Article 20 of the General Data Protection Regulation.[14]The Australian government has recently proposed the introduction of a new "Consumer Data Right", aimed at facilitating data portability to guarantee to consumers the ability to switch and foster competition.[15] In the context of its market study on digital comparison tools, the UK Competition and Markets Authority (CMA) has recommended exploring the use of data portability to foster competition between these online tools (CMA, 2017a, p. 84).

5.4.2. Financial consumer protection regulation and enforcement

Financial services regulation illustrates the role that sector-specific regulation can play in promoting trust in online markets. Among many other things, critical component is ensuring that oversight bodies, i.e. regulatory or supervisory authorities charged with protecting financial consumers, have adequate supervisory tools and the right mix of resources and capabilities to be able to respond appropriately to new digital business and distribution models.

A key consideration for such oversight bodies is to achieve a balance between the development of technological innovation without undue limitation and ensuring that an appropriate level of financial consumer protection is maintained. Depending on the circumstances, approaches may include establishing mechanisms such as "regulatory sandboxes" to allow new business models to be tested in a controlled environment, "innovation hubs", applying proportionate regulatory requirements and/or providing regulatory support, advice or guidance on the application of the regulatory framework.

Requirements relating to disclosure and transparency are a fundamental part of most financial consumer protection regimes. Technological developments, including the availability of data, provide opportunities to improve disclosure approaches based on a better understanding of consumer decision-making and to explore alternatives. Approaches for consideration by policymakers include, *inter alia*:

- Testing and exploring new ways of making disclosure more effective for consumers in terms of more targeted, proportionate and customer-centric approaches. For example, when designing their online finance platforms or applications, banks in Hong Kong, China should consider the use of tools such as pop-ups and hyper-linked text to provide customers with information to help them to make informed borrowing decisions.
- Encouraging financial services providers to test digital disclosure approaches to ensure their effectiveness, taking into account factors such as different screen sizes, communication formats, different local languages and dialects and the digital

literacy of the target audience for the product. For example, findings from a recent European Commission (2019) study shows that information provided upfront, saliently, early enough in the process, in an engaging format and in a way that aids comparison helps consumers make better choices online, especially those that are vulnerable due to their low digital and financial literacy. The study also confirms that presenting the information in a way that is adapted to the size of mobile screens helps consumers make better choices.

- Technological developments and the increasing availability and use of data also have the potential to create opportunities to explore alternatives to disclosure, for example, via the publication of indicators relating to financial products or services; "smart defaults" where consumers are defaulted to a particular option; or "personalised friction" which allows customers to create steps which act as breaks in a financial transaction.

In relation to the provision of advice, including digital advice, approaches for consideration by policymakers include ensuring that algorithms underlying the generation of digital advice are objective and consistent, and that the methodology underpinning digital advice services is clear and transparent, including options for recourse.

5.4.3. Competition law enforcement

While promoting trust in markets is not an explicit primary goal of competition law, efforts to tackle misconduct or anticompetitive transactions could be broadly beneficial for trust. In particular, enforcement action that protects competition helps ensure that less trustworthy firms are driven out of markets, and new business models that emphasise consumer trust (e.g. data protection-focused offerings) can emerge.

One circumstance in which competition enforcement promotes trust in online markets is when the determinants of trust, such as privacy protections, can be considered elements of quality for the purposes of competition analysis. For instance, and notwithstanding the fact that to date no such case seems to have been brought to the attention of competition authority, the level of privacy or data protection could be limited as a result of a collusive practice by competing companies.

Similarly, the degradation of privacy, data protection or advertisement policies and reduced choice could be the result of an abuse by a dominant firm. Exclusionary strategies may prevent new firms that emphasise privacy protections from emerging. For example, some authors argue that data portability restrictions by firms could qualify as an abuse of a dominant position *"if it can be proved that the dominant company limits markets and technical development to the prejudice of consumers"* (Vanberg and Unver, 2017; Geradin and Kuschewsky, 2016).

Another enforcement example is the German Bundeskartellamt's decision in the *Facebook* case, where the competition authority stated that *"the extent to which Facebook collects, merges and uses data in user accounts constitutes an abuse of a dominant position"*. The decision, focusing on the use of data obtained by Facebook from affiliated companies, such as Instagram, WhatsApp or other websites, rather than on the exclusionary impact on competitors, requires Facebook to i) request user consent for Facebook-owned services to assign collected data to Facebook user accounts; and ii) request user consent for collecting data from other third party websites and assigning them to a Facebook user account.[16]

A worsening of privacy terms and conditions, an increase in advertising content or reduced choices may also be the result of a merger. However, there may be challenges associated with adopting the right analytical tools for the assessment of mergers effects between online players. One example is the quantification of market shares in zero-price markets, where alternative measures such as the share of users or user interactions may be considered (OECD, 2018b, p. 15). Authorities also face the challenge of assessing mergers that may affect data privacy as one of the possible parameters of competition. For instance, in its decision on *Microsoft/LinkedIn*,[17] the European Commission concluded that the merger could lead to a substantial reduction in consumer choice for professional networks, including with respect to privacy protection. Specifically, the Commission found there were risks that competitors offering better privacy protection could be marginalised following the merger, and therefore required remedies to address these concerns.

5.4.4. Interdisciplinary regulator cooperation and advocacy

The objective of promoting informed trust among consumers in online markets cannot be achieved through a single policy lens, nor will the enforcement of existing rules address all of the concerns and risks outlined above. The OECD E-commerce Recommendation (OECD, 2016b) contains key provisions aimed to build consumer trust in online markets and ensure that consumers benefit from fair business and advertising practices, appropriate disclosures, effective processes for transaction confirmation and payment, measures to address privacy and security risks, product safety, and meaningful access to effective mechanisms to resolve disputes. Other instruments such as the OECD Privacy Guidelines (OECD, 2013) and the OECD Digital Security Risk Management Recommendation (OECD, 2015) underscore the necessity of a coordinated approach to tackle problems arising in online markets, e.g. the security of digital identity in online transactions, digital risk insurance, data governance, data access and portability and algorithmic discrimination (Donohue et al., 2017).

First, there are opportunities for competition, consumer protection, data protection and sector regulatory authorities to coordinate their enforcement efforts by exchanging information, producing joint guidance for the industry, or promoting initiatives aimed at supporting one another in investigations and case management (OECD, 2018b). These opportunities for collaboration can be exploited to promote engaged decision-making by consumers and foster informed trust. For example, competition law remedies aimed at better informing and empowering consumers could be designed with the advice of consumer or data protection authorities. In relation to digital markets, the OECD advocated close cooperation between different authorities in its Recommendation of the Council on Cross-Border Cooperation in the Enforcement of Laws against Spam (OECD, 2006), as did the European Data Protection Supervisor in its 2014 Preliminary Opinion of Privacy and Competitiveness in the Age of Big Data.[18]

Second, regulators can cooperate in terms of their advocacy efforts aimed at better informing consumers and firms. Initiatives to address the asymmetry of information in online markets that have a negative impact on the level of trust could include information campaigns aimed at educating consumers about personal data and privacy. An example for which consumer education is particularly important, and which could benefit from multidisciplinary cooperation, is the financial sector (see Box 5.2).

One advocacy tool that could be particularly effective in identifying issues contributing to trust problems in online markets, and which could serve as a platform for interdisciplinary cooperation, is a market study. Market studies, often carried out by competition authorities, are used when competition law enforcement action is not warranted, but competition does not seem to be functioning properly. They could be used to diagnose problems in markets and their causes, whether these are related to market failures (including information asymmetries), demand-side problems, unintended consequences of regulation, or firm conduct that is not illegal but which raises policy concerns, among others. Measures to address competition, consumer protection or data protection concerns could be designed, including further advocacy aimed at firms or consumers, or recommendations for policy changes by governments. In a small number of jurisdictions, competition authorities also have powers to impose remedies in the context of a market study. These have been used, for example, to improve the information available to consumers, reduce switching costs, and encourage new entry (OECD, 2018c, p. 4). The German competition authority (Bundeskartellamt) has, for example, recently obtained legislative powers to initiate market studies in cases where substantial consumer protection concerns are identified.[19]

Box 5.2. Consumer financial education measures

In terms of financial education strategies aimed at supporting consumers to become digitally and financially literate, policymakers should develop core competencies frameworks and appropriate financial education material that can contribute to:

- Build trust and promote beneficial use of DFS and related technological innovation.
- Protect consumers and small businesses from vulnerability to digital crime and misuse/mis-selling.
- Empower consumers to counter new types of exclusion due to the potential misuse of data sources, including data analytics and digital profiling.
- Support consumers at risk of over-reliance on easy access to online sources of credit.

Based on these core competencies, the authorities responsible for financial education, in cooperation with relevant stakeholders, should support the effective delivery of financial education through digital and traditional means and address the needs of target audiences through tailored approaches. This should be undertaken in particular by exploiting the advantages of digital delivery.

Digital tools can also improve access to financial education by, for example, making it more affordable and accessible by wider audiences and tailoring financial education to individual needs, through the possibility of setting up profiles or accounts on digital platforms and obtaining personalised information, instruction and advice. (See OECD, 2017c for further resources.)

An example of a market study which dealt with issues of both competition and trust is the UK retail banking market investigation. The UK CMA required banks to implement Open Banking standards (through common digital protocols, called application programme interfaces, or APIs for short) to enable consumers to make more use of their personal financial information and use it, for example, to better manage their money, or to compare products and services on the basis of their individual needs. The success of these remedies hinged largely on consumer trust, as retail banking customers could choose for their data to be shared with selected third parties such as digital comparison tools or money management apps to take advantage of their services without fearing that it would be compromised.[20] Well-established data governance standards, alongside effective regulation of the selected third parties, was therefore a particular focus.

Third, and finally, interdisciplinary cooperation may be needed to design additional regulatory policy measures when existing enforcement tools and advocacy efforts are not sufficient. For example, the market failures, consumer biases and distortions (e.g. switching costs) described above may prevent market competition from meeting consumer demands.

Regulation and policies can be designed to promote trust through two mechanisms: first, setting the limits of the competitive playing field for firms, allowing consumers to have confidence that, for example, their personal data will be subject to protections and limitations over undue or abusive use via proper data governance; and second, stimulating competition by giving consumers meaningful opportunities to make choices. Potential options may include, for example, the adoption of more protective policies as a default option, or policies that require websites to provide consumers with opt-in instead of opt-out options for data collection (Kerber, 2016, p. 862). Consumer protection policies could benefit from a competition lens to ensure a level playing field, for example between traditional banks and technology firms seeking to provide financial services.

In the longer term, measures to promote more effective online disclosures (see OECD, 2018e), and more comprehensive consumer options that enable an assessment of trade-offs by consumers, are crucial to attain informed trust. For example, in relation to trust issues around personal data, business models could be encouraged that offer a menu of options, such as a premium option that involves a high price in return for limited data collection, a middle of the road option that limits data use, and a discount option that provides free, or even negatively-priced services, in exchange for wide-ranging data use. Designing new regulatory measures will require a careful assessment of likely consumer and firm behavioural responses, and a mix of regulatory perspectives.

Any new regulatory or policy measure should avoid hampering the introduction of trust-enhancing innovations by businesses themselves. As mentioned above, significant innovations are being developed by businesses to foster trust and gain or re-gain consumers' confidence, for instance by applying new technologies to restore control over personal data (see the Tide Foundation example above) or developing solutions to facilitate data portability.[21]

5.5. Conclusions

Online markets offer a host of benefits for consumers by providing with greater choices of new, innovative and often cheaper products. However, these markets cannot fulfil their potential if consumers are unable to trust them. Where product information is hard to obtain and assess, markets may not respond to consumers' needs. Misaligned incentives, information asymmetries and consumer behavioural biases, such as the free effect, the privacy paradox and the inhibiting power of the status quo, can exacerbate these risks.

An atmosphere of informed trust must therefore be a key objective of policymakers. The consequences of a lack of informed trust could stem from two sources: insufficient trust that stifles growth in online markets, with broader economic effects; and blind implicit trust, that makes individual consumers susceptible to misconduct while hampering the ability of competition to deliver the best products and services (evaluated on a range of parameters including, potentially, privacy protection).

To foster informed trust in these markets, it is important that effective competition, consumer protection, and data protection laws are in place and adequately enforced. Enforcement tools alone, however, may not be sufficient to address the online market failures. Cooperation between competition, data and consumer protection authorities, as well as advocacy activity aimed at promoting procompetitive regulatory reform and private initiatives may be crucial in order for consumers to trust that online markets can offer them a fair deal.

Notes

[1] When referring to online markets for the purposes of this Chapter, reference is made to markets where e-commerce products and services are offered to a final consumer. E-commerce in this narrow sense encompasses the purchase and sale online of goods and services such as tangible goods, services for offline consumption (such as hotel bookings and purchase of tickets) and digital content, with the exclusion, for instance, of intermediation services to online retailers or online marketing activities (OECD, 2018, p. 6).

[2] "An e-commerce transaction is the sale or purchase of goods or services, conducted over computer networks by methods specifically designed for the purpose of receiving or placing of orders. The goods or services are ordered by those methods, but the payment and the ultimate delivery of the goods or services do not have to be conducted online. An e-commerce transaction can be between enterprises, households, individuals, governments, and other public or private organisations." OECD (2011), p. 72.

[3] This definition of trust in online markets is based on the definition proposed by R. C. Mayer, J. H. Davis and F. D. Schoorman (1995), "An Integrative Model of Organizational Trust", *20 The Academy of Management Review* 3, 709-734, p. 712, as "the willingness of a party to be vulnerable to the actions of another party based on the expectation that the other will perform a particular action important to the trustor, irrespective of the ability to monitor or control that other party".

[4] For instance, at the early stages of the commercial development of the internet, D. L. Hoffman, T. P. Novak and M. Peralta (1999), "Building Consumer Trust in Online Environments: The Case for Information Privacy", *42 Communications of the ACM* 4, 80-85, p. 80, noted that *"the reason online consumers have yet to shop online in large numbers, or even provide information to Web providers in exchange for access to information offered onsite, is because of the fundamental lack of faith that currently exists between most businesses and consumers on the Web today. In essence, consumers simply do not trust most Web providers enough to engage in relationship exchanges with them".* The environment changed, of course, but trust remained a fundamental element in the interaction between internet users and providers.

[5] President's Council of Advisors on Science and Technology (2014), "Report to the President – Big Data and Privacy: A Technological Perspective", https://obamawhitehouse.archives.gov/sites/default/files/microsites/ostp/PCAST/pcast_big_data_and_privacy_-_may_2014.pdf, p. 12.

[6] The Guardian (2014), "Italy Fines TripAdvisor €500,000 over False Reviews", https://www.theguardian.com/travel/2014/dec/23/italy-fines-tripadvisor-500000?CMP=aff_1432&awc=5795_1546443330_f62e3f3221f225ded14706ebf1b5dd82; S. Fenton (2015), "TripAdvisor Denies Rating System is Flawed, After Fake Restaurant Tops Rankings in Italy", www.independent.co.uk/life-style/gadgets-and-tech/news/tripadvisor-denies-rating-system-is-flawed-after-fake-restaurant-tops-rankings-in-italy-10354818.html.

[7] The Guardian (2018), "Meriton Fined $3m for Manipulating TripAdvisor Hotel Reviews", www.theguardian.com/travel/2018/jul/31/meriton-fined-3m-for-manipulating-tripadvisor-hotel-reviews.

[8] Reuters (2018), "Man Jailed in Italy for Writing Fake TripAdvisor Review, www.reuters.com/article/us-italy-tripadvisor/man-jailed-in-italy-for-writing-fake-tripadvisor-review-company-idUSKCN1LS2S3.

[9] https://www.gov.uk/cma-cases/potential-fake-online-reviews-search-engine-optimisation-company.

[10] UK Competition and Market Authority case on Social Media Endorsements, www.gov.uk/cma-cases/social-media-endorsements.

[11] The Guardian (2018), "Man Jailed in Italy for Selling Fake TripAdvisor Reviews", www.theguardian.com/world/2018/sep/12/man-jailed-italy-selling-fake-tripadvisor-reviews-promo-salento. TripAdvisor allows users to mark with a grey flag reviews that seem suspicious or in violation of the website's guidelines, for more information, see www.tripadvisorsupport.com/hc/en-us/articles/200614937-How-do-I-report-an-inappropriate-review-.

[12] G20-OECD Task Force on Consumer Protection, www.oecd.org/finance/g20-oecd-task-force-financial-consumer-protection.htm.

[13] See, for instance, L. Zingales and G. Rolnik (2017), "A Way to Own Your Social-Media Data", *New York Times*, www.nytimes.com/2017/06/30/opinion/social-data-google-facebook-europe.html; W. Kerber (2016), "Digital markets, data, and privacy: competition law, consumer law and data protection", 11 *Journal of Intellectual Property Law & Practice* 1, https://doi.org/10.1093/jiplp/jpw150, p. 862- 863; G. Colangelo and M. Maggiolino (2018), "Data Accumulation and the Privacy-Antitrust Interface: Insights from the Facebook case for the EU and the U.S.", *Stanford-Vienna Transatlantic Technology Law Forum Working Papers*, No. 31, p. 11.

[14] Article 20 of Regulation (EU) 2016/679 of the European Parliament and of the Council of 27 April 2016 on the protection of natural persons with regard to the processing of personal data and on the free movement of such data, and repealing Directive 95/46/EC (General Data Protection Regulation) http://data.europa.eu/eli/reg/2016/679/oj.

[15] See https://treasury.gov.au/consumer-data-right/ and C. Beaton-Wells (2018), "Platform Power and Privacy Protection: A Case for Policy Innovation", *CPI Antitrust Chronicle*, pp. 6-8.

[16] Press Release www.bundeskartellamt.de/SharedDocs/Meldung/EN/Pressemitteilungen/2019/07_02_2019_Facebook.html and decision of the Bundeskartellamt, 6 February 2019, www.bundeskartellamt.de/SharedDocs/Entscheidung/EN/Fallberichte/Missbrauchsaufsicht/2019/B6-22-16.pdf.

[17] European Commission , 6 December 2016, COMP/M.8124 – Microsoft/LinkedIn, http://ec.europa.eu/competition/mergers/cases/decisions/m8124_1349_5.pdf

[18] European Data Protection Supervisor (2014), "Privacy and Competitiveness in the Age of Big Data: the Interplay between Data Protection, Competition Law and Consumer Protection in the Digital Economy", https://edps.europa.eu/sites/edp/files/publication/14-03-26_competitition_law_big_data_en.pdf.

[19] 9th Amendment to the German Competition Act, see for information https://www.bundeskartellamt.de/SharedDocs/Meldung/EN/Pressemitteilungen/2017/12_06_2017_Abteilung%20V.html.

[20] UK Competition and Markets Authority Open Banking, www.openbanking.org.uk/about-us/.

[21] See, for example, the Data Transfer Project, https://datatransferproject.dev/.

References

Acquisti, A., L. Brandimarte, G. Loewenstein (2015), "Privacy and Human Behaviour in the Age of Information" *Science,* Vol. 347/6221, pp. 509-514.

Beaton-Wells, C. (2018), "Platform Power and Privacy Protection: A Case for Policy Innovation", *CPI Antitrust Chronicle*.

Ben-Sahar, O. (2008), "The Myth of the 'Opportunity to Read' in Contract Law"*, Law &Economics Working Papers*, http://chicagounbound.uchicago.edu/law_and_economics/549.

Chun, S.-H. (2019), "E-Commerce Liability and Security Breaches in Mobile Payment for e-Business Sustainability", *Sustainability*, vol. 11, p. 13, doi: 3390/su11030715.

CMA (2017a), Digital Comparison Tool Market Study – Final Report, Competition and Markets Authority, https://assets.publishing.service.gov.uk/media/59c93546e5274a77468120d6/digital-comparison-tools-market-study-final-report.pdf.

CMA (2017b), Digital Comparison Tool Market Study – Final Report – Paper A: Consumer Views, Behaviour, and Experiences, Competition and Markets Authority, https://assets.publishing.service.gov.uk/media/59c9356bed915d7bd5d75dda/paper-a-consumer-experiences.pdf.

CMA (2015), "The Commercial Use of Consumer Data - Report on the CMA's call for information", Competition and Markets Authority, https://assets.publishing.service.gov.uk/government/uploads/system/uploads/attachment_data/file/435817/The_commercial_use_of_consumer_data.pdf.

Colangelo, G. and M. Maggiolino (2018), "Data Accumulation and the Privacy-Antitrust Interface: Insights from the Facebook case for the EU and the U.S.", *Stanford-Vienna Transatlantic Technology Law Forum Working Papers*, No. 31.

DMA (2012), "Data Privacy: What the Consumer Really Thinks", Direct Marketing Association, https://dma.org.uk/uploads/Data%20privacy%20-%20What%20the%20consumer%20really%20thinks%202012_53cfd432518f2.pdf.

Donohue, M., E. Ronchi and L. Bernat (2016), "Bridging policy silos to boost trust online", *OECD Observer,* http://oecdobserver.org/news/fullstory.php/aid/5589/Bridging_policy_silos_to_boost_trust_online.html.

European Commission (2019), "Behavioural study on the digitalisation of the marketing and distance selling of retail financial services", https://ec.europa.eu/info/sites/info/files/live_work_travel_in_the_eu/consumers/digitalisation_of_financial_services_-_main_report.pdf

European Commission (2015), Special Eurobarometer, Cyber Security Report, http://ec.europa.eu/commfrontoffice/publicopinion/archives/ebs/ebs_423_en.pdf.

Friederiszick, H. W. and E. Głowicka (2016), "Competition Policy in Modern Retail Markets", *Journal of Antitrust Enforcement,* Vol.4/1, pp. 42-83, https://doi.org/10.1093/jaenfo/jnv030.

Gabaix, X. and D. Laibson (2005), "Shrouded Attributes, Consumer Myopia, and Information Suppression in Competitive Markets", *NBER Working Paper Series*, http://www.nber.org/papers/w11755.

Geradin, D. and M. Kuschewsky, "Competition Law and Personal Data: Preliminary Thoughts on a Complex Issue", https://ssrn.com/abstract=2216088.

Grabner-Kraeuter, S. (2002), "The Role of Consumers' Trust in Online-Shopping", *Journal of Business Ethics*, Vol. 39, pp. 43-50.

Head, M. M. and K. Hassanein (2001), "Trust in e-Commerce: Evaluating the Impact of Third-Party Seals", http://citeseerx.ist.psu.edu/viewdoc/download?doi=10.1.1.465.9764&rep=rep1&type=pdf.

Hoffman, D. L., T. P. Novak and M. Peralta (1999), "Building Consumer Trust in Online Environments: The Case for Information Privacy", *Communications of the ACM,* Vol. 42/4, pp. 80-85.

Kerber, W. (2016), "Digital markets, data, and privacy: competition law, consumer law and data protection", 11 *Journal of Intellectual Property Law & Practice* 1, https://doi.org/10.1093/jiplp/jpw150.

Madden, M. (2014), "Public Perceptions of Privacy and Security in the Post-Snowden Era – Summary of Findings", *Pew Research Centre Information and Technology,* www.pewinternet.org/2014/11/12/public-privacy-perceptions/.

Mayer, R.C., J. H. Davis and F. D. Schoorman (1995), "An Integrative Model of Organizational Trust", 20 *The Academy of Management Review* 3, 709-734.

McDonald, A. M. and L. F. Cranor (2008), "The Cost of Reading Privacy Policies" *A Journal of Law and Policy for the Information Society,* Vol. 4/3, https://kb.osu.edu/bitstream/handle/1811/72839/ISJLP_V4N3_543.pdf.

Murray, A. (2016), *Information Technology Law*, 3rd ed., Oxford University Press.

Nicolau, J. L. and R. Sellers (2012), "The Free Breakfast Effect: An Experimental Approach to the Zero Price Model in Tourism", *Journal of Travel Research*, Vol. 51/3, pp. 243-249.

OECD (2019a), "Roundtable on Online Consumer Reviews: Committee on Consumer Policy Summary of Discussion", https://one.oecd.org/document/DSTI/CP(2019)8/FINAL/en/pdf.

OECD (2019b), "Going Digital, Shaping Policies, Improving Lives", https://doi.org/10.1787/9789264312012-en.

OECD (2019c), "Online Advertising: Trends, Benefits and Risks for Consumers", *OECD Digital Economy Papers No. 272,* https://doi.org/10.1787/1f42c85d-en .

OECD (2019d), *OECD SME and Entrepreneurship Outlook 2019*, OECD Publishing, Paris, https://doi.org/10.1787/34907e9c-en.

OECD (2018a), "Implications of E-Commerce for Competition Policy", DAF/COMP(2018)3, https://one.oecd.org/document/DAF/COMP(2018)3/en/pdf.

OECD (2018b), "Quality Considerations in Digital Zero-Price Markets", DAF/COMP(2018)14, https://one.oecd.org/document/DAF/COMP(2018)14/en/pdf.

OECD (2018c), "Guide on Market Studies for Competition Authorities", DAF/COMP/WD(2018)26, https://one.oecd.org/document/DAF/COMP/WD(2018)26/en/pdf.

OECD (2018d), "Personalised Pricing in the Digital Era", DAF/COMP(2018)13, https://one.oecd.org/document/DAF/COMP(2018)13/en/pdf.

OECD (2018e), "Improving online disclosures with behavioural insights", *OECD Digital Economy Papers*, No. 269, OECD Publishing, Paris, https://doi.org/10.1787/39026ff4-en.

OECD (2018f), "Toolkit for Protecting Digital Consumers: A Resource for G20 Policy Makers", www.oecd.org/internet/consumer/toolkit-for-protecting-digital-consumers.pdf.

OECD (2018g), *G20/OECD Policy Guidance on Digitalisation and Financial Literacy,* www.oecd.org/finance/G20-OECD-INFE-Policy-Guidance-Digitalisation-Financial-Literacy-2018.pdf.

OECD (2018h), *G20/OECD Policy Guidance on Financial Consumer Protection Approaches in the Digital Age,* www.oecd.org/finance/G20-OECD-Policy-Guidance-Financial-Consumer-Protection-Digital-Age-2018.pdf.

OECD (2017a), *OECD Digital Economy Outlook 2017*, https://doi.org/10.1787/9789264276284-en.

OECD (2017b), "Going Digital: Making the Transformation Work for Growth and Well-Being", www.oecd.org/mcm/documents/C-MIN-2017-4%20EN.pdf.

OECD (2017c), "G20/OECD INFE report on adult financial literacy in G20 countries", www.oecd.org/daf/fin/financial-education/G20-OECD-INFE-report-adult-financial-literacy-in-G20-countries.pdf.

OECD (2016a), "Consumer Protection in E-commerce: OECD Recommendation", OECD Publishing, Paris, http://dx.doi.org/10.1787/9789264255258-en.

OECD (2016b), "Protecting Consumers in Peer Platform Markets: Exploring the Issues", OECD Digital Economy Papers, No. 253, https://doi.org/10.1787/5jlwvz39m1zw-en.

OECD (2015), *Digital Security Risk Management for Economic and Social Prosperity: OECD Recommendation and Companion Document*, OECD Publishing, Paris, https://doi.org/10.1787/9789264245471-en.

OECD (2013), The OECD Privacy Framework, including the OECD Guidelines on the Protection of Privacy and Transborder Flows of Personal Data", www.oecd.org/internet/ieconomy/privacy-guidelines.htm.

OECD (2012), The Digital Economy, DAF/COMP(2012)22, www.oecd.org/daf/competition/The-Digital-Economy-2012.pdf.

OECD (2011), OECD Guide to Measuring the Information Society 2011, OECD Publishing, Paris, http://dx.doi.org/10.1787/10.1787/9789264113541-en,

OECD (2010), OECD Consumer Policy Toolkit, https://doi.org/10.1787/9789264079663-en.

OECD (2006), "Recommendation of the Council on Cross-Border Cooperation in the Enforcement of Laws against Spam", OECD/LEGAL/0344, https://legalinstruments.oecd.org/public/doc/118/118.en.pdf.

OECD (2002), *OECD Guidelines on the Protection of Privacy and Transborder Flows of Personal Data*, OECD Publishing, Paris, https://doi.org/10.1787/9789264196391-en.

PwC (2018), "Global Top 100 companies by market capitalisation: 31 March 2018 update", www.pwc.com/gx/en/audit-services/assets/pdf/global-top-100-companies-2018-report.pdf.

PwC (2017), Consumer Intelligence Series: Protect.me An in-depth look at what consumers want, what worries them, and how companies can earn their trust—and their business, www.pwc.com/us/en/services/consulting/library/consumer-intelligence-series/cybersecurity-protect-me.html.

Shampan'er K. and D. Ariely (2016), "How Small is Zero-price? The True Value of Free Products", *Federal Reserve Bank of Boston Working Papers*, No. 06-16, www.bostonfed.org/-/media/Documents/Workingpapers/PDF/wp0616.pdf.

Shampan'er K., N. Mazar and D. Ariely (2007), "Zero as a Special Price: The True Value of Free Products", *Marketing Science*, Vol. 26/6, www-2.rotman.utoronto.ca/facbios/file/ZeroPrice.pdf, pp. 742–757.

Shapiro, J. (2018), "Tide Foundation pitches blockchain solution to digital advertising privacy woes", *Financial Review*, www.afr.com/business/media-and-marketing/advertising/the-tide-turns-the-elegant-blockchain-solution-to-20180822-h14cmm.

Statista (2019a), Retail e-commerce sales worldwide from 2014 to 2021, www.statista.com/statistics/379046/worldwide-retail-e-commerce-sales/

Statista (2019b), Digital buyers worldwide from 2014 to 2021, www.statista.com/statistics/251666/number-of-digital-buyers-worldwide/.

Stucke, M. and A. Ezrachi (2016), "When Competition Fails to Optimize Quality: A Look at Search Engines", *Yale Journal of Law and Technology*, Vol 18/70, https://papers.ssrn.com/sol3/papers.cfm?abstract_id=2598128.

Stucke, M. E. and A. P. Grunes (2016), *Big Data and Competition Policy*, Oxford University Press.

Tsai, J. Y., S. Egelman, L. Cranor, A. Acquisti (2011), "The Effect of Online Privacy Information on Purchasing Behaviour: An Experimental Study", *Information Systems Research*, Vol. 22/2, https://pdfs.semanticscholar.org/e221/d15a4b9f2eb2ab07694aaa584bd59c85532c.pdf, 254-268.

Turow, J., M. Hennessy, and N. Draper (2015), "The Tradeoff Fallacy: How Marketers Are Misrepresenting American Consumers and Opening Them Up to Exploitation", www.asc.upenn.edu/sites/default/files/TradeoffFallacy_1.pdf.

Vanberg, A. D., M. B. Unver (2017), "The right to data portability in the GDPR and EU competition law: off couple or dynamic duo", *European Journal of Law and Technology*, Vol. 8/1.

Woollacott, E. (2017), "Amazon's Fake Review Problem is No Worse than Ever, Study Suggests", www.forbes.com/sites/emmawoollacott/2017/09/09/exclusive-amazons-fake-review-problem-is-now-worse-than-ever/#32b58b247c0f.

Zingales, L. and G. Rolnik (2017), "A Way to Own Your Social-Media Data", *New York Times*, www.nytimes.com/2017/06/30/opinion/social-data-google-facebook-europe.html.

ORGANISATION FOR ECONOMIC CO-OPERATION AND DEVELOPMENT

The OECD is a unique forum where governments work together to address the economic, social and environmental challenges of globalisation. The OECD is also at the forefront of efforts to understand and to help governments respond to new developments and concerns, such as corporate governance, the information economy and the challenges of an ageing population. The Organisation provides a setting where governments can compare policy experiences, seek answers to common problems, identify good practice and work to co-ordinate domestic and international policies.

The OECD member countries are: Australia, Austria, Belgium, Canada, Chile, the Czech Republic, Denmark, Estonia, Finland, France, Germany, Greece, Hungary, Iceland, Ireland, Israel, Italy, Japan, Korea, Latvia, Lithuania, Luxembourg, Mexico, the Netherlands, New Zealand, Norway, Poland, Portugal, the Slovak Republic, Slovenia, Spain, Sweden, Switzerland, Turkey, the United Kingdom and the United States. The European Union takes part in the work of the OECD.

OECD Publishing disseminates widely the results of the Organisation's statistics gathering and research on economic, social and environmental issues, as well as the conventions, guidelines and standards agreed by its members.

OECD PUBLISHING, 2, rue André-Pascal, 75775 PARIS CEDEX 16
ISBN 978-92-64-50714-2 – 2019

www.ingramcontent.com/pod-product-compliance
Ingram Content Group UK Ltd.
Pitfield, Milton Keynes, MK11 3LW, UK
UKHW051505290926
15471UKWH00008B/1424

9 789264 507142